Missouri Memories
(1934-1947)

Missouri Memories
(1934-1947)

Thomas H. Olbricht

INTRODUCTION BY Kathy J. Pulley

AFTERWORD BY Brooks Blevins

RESOURCE *Publications* · Eugene, Oregon

MISSOURI MEMORIES (1934–1947)

Copyright © 2016 Thomas H. Olbricht. All rights reserved. Except for brief quotations in critical publications or reviews, no part of this book may be reproduced in any manner without prior written permission from the publisher. Write: Permissions, Wipf and Stock Publishers, 199 W. 8th Ave., Suite 3, Eugene, OR 97401.

Resource Publications
An Imprint of Wipf and Stock Publishers
199 W. 8th Ave., Suite 3
Eugene, OR 97401

www.wipfandstock.com

PAPERBACK ISBN: 978-1-4982-9460-7
HARDCOVER ISBN: 978-1-4982-9462-1
EBOOK ISBN: 978-1-4982-9461-4

Manufactured in the U.S.A.   07/12/16

Some of the material in the Introduction, and especially Chapter III and elsewhere has been published in; Thomas H. Olbricht, *Reflections on My Life in the Kingdom and the Academy* (Eugene, OR,: Wipf and Stock, 2012) and reprinted by permission.

Chapter III is slightly revised from an essay: Thomas H. Olbricht, "Recalling Ozarks Past: Winter 1936," *OzarksWatch*, Series 2, III, 2, pp. 12–25. Reprinted by permission.

Chapter VI Some of this information may be found in my essay, Thomas H. Olbricht, "The Arrival of the Churches of Christ in Randolph & Fulton Counties, Arkansas, and in Oregon Country Missouri," *OzarksWatch*, Series 2, III, 1, pp. 74–88.

Some of what is in Chapter VII may be found in my essay, Thomas H. Olbricht, "Restoration Revivalism in Oregon Country, Missouri, and Fulton County, Arkansas, 1930-1950)" *Elder Mountain: A Journal of Ozarks Studies*, Vol. 4, 2012, 88–108. Reprinted by permission.

The material in Chapters VIII and IX somewhat revised were published in Thomas H. Olbricht, "Navigating War and Peace: 1943—1947 in the Ozarks," *OzarksWatch*, Series 2, Vol. IV, No. 2, pp. 9–47 and reprinted by permission.

This book is dedicated to the memory of my maternal Grandparents Thomas Shelton Taylor (1876–1968) and Myrtle May Dunsmore Taylor (1879–1969) with whom I lived from 1937–1943.

Contents

Acknowledgments | ix
Introduction by Kathy J. Pulley | xi

CHAPTER I
Memories Embellished? | 1

CHAPTER II
A Depression Child | 8

CHAPTER III
Ozark Christmas in 1936 | 23

CHAPTER IV
Later Depression Years | 43

CHAPTER V
Childhood Activities | 57

CHAPTER VI
My Religious Upbringing | 72

CHAPTER VII
Missouri Evangelism | 89

CHAPTER VIII
War | 100

CHAPTER IX
Peace | 118

Afterword by Brooks Blevins | 135
Images | 137
Bibliography | 149
Name Index | 153

Acknowledgments

First of all I am indebted to Professor Kathy J. Pulley of the Department of Religious Studies at Missouri State University. Kathy encouraged me some years ago to publish a book on my Missouri experiences. In 2008 she invited me to present a lecture at the fall Ozark Festival on the Missouri State campus facilitating further my intent to publish either essays or perhaps a book. I first met Kathy at Abilene Christian University where I became her graduate advisor and MA thesis director. It didn't take us long to discover that actually, though we are not related, our families are intertwined through marriages. I am also indebted to Brooks Blevins of the Department of History and Missouri State University for his Afterword. He is especially focused upon Ozark Studies in his teaching and publications.

My mother and her five siblings attended Missouri State University all of whom received a baccalaureate degree except for Norval R. Taylor who in the early 1930s as a college junior was appointed the bulk agent of Standard Oil of Indiana for Oregon County Missouri, a position he deemed wise in the heart of the depression not to turn down. My aunts and uncles graduated from what was then Southwest State Teachers College in the 1920s and 1930s. My mother, Agnes Martha Taylor Olbricht (1898–1978) was the oldest. The others were: Bertha May Taylor Lewis (1901–1989), Norval Ray Taylor (1905–1977), Cleo Shelt Taylor (1907–1994), Alice Nora Taylor Copenhagen (1909–1987), and Wellington Thomas Taylor (1917–1993). Bertha, Cleo, Alice and Wellington additionally all attended the University of Missouri in order to qualify for vocational agriculture and home economics teaching programs. My mother taught in Missouri schools, first in high school and later in an elementary school. Bertha and Alice were Vocational Home Economic teachers in Missouri schools. Cleo and Wellington

Acknowledgments

(Tom) were Vocational Agriculture teachers in Missouri. Later Cleo served as a principal and Wellington took a position with Carnation Milk as a milk tester, and later became a plant manager in Mt Vernon.

Various persons have read materials in this book and made suggestions including my wife Dorothy, Kathy Pulley, Bill and Patty Henegar, Cleone McGinness, Max Evans, Bob Friedman, and Owen Olbricht. Max, Bob and Owen all grew up in Thayer, Missouri. I am also indebted to Brooks Blevins and John Smalzbauer of the Missouri State Faculty for comments on materials in chapters V and VI and to C. D. Albin, editor of the *Elder Mountain: A Journal of Ozark Studies* Published by Missouri State University, West Plains, for his editorial work on materials found in chapters V and VI. To all of these readers and editors I am deeply indebted for invaluable suggestions. Special thanks go to Erika M. Olbricht for reading the proofs.

Introduction

It was the mid-1970s, about 2:50 p.m. on an early September day, when I sat down in my first graduate class at Abilene Christian University. I didn't want to be late for the 3:00 p.m. start of this three-hour class. Unlike my undergraduate experiences at a state university, the students who started coming into this class, "Introduction to Doctrines," were all males and they all seemed to know each other. I had all the "first-day jitters." Would I "fit" into a master's program in theological studies? Southwest Texas seemed a far distance from my home in southwest Missouri. Professor Thomas Olbricht entered the room and without much ado started making preliminary comments. In the opening moments he called attention to me. Maybe he introduced others, but I do not recall. What I do remember is that he took a moment to introduce me to the class. His exact words escape my memory, but he successfully communicated that I was from the Ozarks, and that he and I might even be related (we are related by marriage if not by blood). He went on to say that my parents had grown up very close to his own family roots in Thayer, Missouri. In those few ordinary words, and in his soft gestures and expressions I felt welcomed by him. I relaxed. After all, he was my advisor, and through that welcome I felt like I really was a part of his extended family—I was "in." And so we began a relationship that now spans more than forty years. He and I share common roots, but he welcomed every other of his many students in some brief, genuine way, without flair. That was his way, and that is the way hospitality works in the Ozarks.

In some ways similar to Isak Dinesen's vignettes of Kenya, in *Out of Africa*, Tom's *Missouri Memories* provides detailed snapshots of the first eighteen years of his life and the life of an Ozarks family of the 1930s and 1940s. The major themes are what one might expect: family, faith,

Introduction

education, and community. His brief sketches are rich with details about everyday ordinary life events. He includes accounts about the impact of the Depression, World War II, and how his community celebrated the Christmas of 1936. There are stories about his local Church of Christ and the history of the Churches of Christ. The influence of the people and events of Thayer is great. When the stories come to an end, one feels as familiar with the real town of Thayer as with the fictional Port William after finishing one of Wendell Berry's novels. However, through the short and subtle telling of the stories one realizes the value of the stories: they are not random. They are memories that profoundly shaped the man.

Born in 1929, Tom spent his earliest years living through the Depression. For various reasons, neither Tom's immediate family nor his extended family experienced devastating financial losses or the loss of their jobs. His father was frugal, and on their eleven acres the family grew much of what they ate, and were able to provide for themselves. However, they were not insulated from the effects of the Depression. Sometimes his mother provided food to hobos traveling through by train, and the community women made quilts for those who were in need.

In his first chapter he introduces his family. Unlike many Ozarks families, a good number of Tom's family members were college educated, including his mother. One uncle was both a successful vocational agriculture high school teacher as well as a successful big business farmer. Education was woven into his life through such events as his mother's efforts to read to her four children and their weekly trips to the library. Tom loved reading about Thomas Edison and all his inventions. Among other things, his father read the weekly *Kansas City Grit*, and his mother liked *In His Steps* by Charles Sheldon. His mother also liked reading the Bible; however, his father did not approve—"He thought that reading led to mental problems—especially reading the Bible. My mother, therefore, read the Bible when he was at work."

The importance of school is ever present. Tom's parents sometimes sent him to live with relatives in order for him to have the best education available in that area. In a region in which one-room schools were still prevalent, and getting an eighth-grade education could be the norm, Tom's parents and his extended family set the bar higher. Thus, it is not surprising that Tom developed the desire to learn, teach, and lead, and found his career home in educational institutions.

Introduction

Signs of his personal Christian faith were also developing throughout his childhood years. Despite the fact that Tom devotes about a fourth of this collection to details about the Churches of Christ in the Thayer area and the history of the Restoration Movement, two of his most personal vignettes have to do with his father's baptism and his own baptism. His father was reared Catholic. He always attended the Church of Christ with his family, but he was not baptized until 1938, in the Spring River below the dam at Mammoth Spring. Tom was eight years old. After his father's baptism, he remembers that his dad was "kinder than I had ever seen him." He recalls thinking, "'Can this be my Dad?' but I became accustomed to his change in attitude. No one was more pleased than my mother." Tom's own baptism took place in the summer of 1946, a few months before his seventeenth birthday. One of the most interesting things about his account of this event was why he did it. Yes, he confessed that Christ was the Son of God, and certainly he wanted to be a prayerful person and one who knew the biblical text. However, his baptismal story is in a section titled "Commitment." He does not stress his theological mindset as much as his thinking that if he was going to be a Christian he needed to "clean up [his] act," and "avoid the temptations into which [he] had to some degree plunged." The "degree of plunging" seems limited, but that is not to suggest that the things he mentioned were not serious issues to him. Like his father, Tom understood that his own baptism called for living a transformed life.

Ultimately, Tom did not major in agriculture as some in the family had planned. Somewhere between Harding College and when I first met him at Abilene, he had become quite the scholar and the churchman. It does not seem possible to separate his scholarship from his life as a churchman, and it is certainly not possible to separate his life as a churchman from the rest of his life. He is a consummate churchman with profound dedication to the Church of Christ tradition. As a student of his, I was drawn to the depth of his scholarship and to its breadth: from biblical theology to restoration history to biblical studies to rhetoric. Much of his writing has direct relevance to the church.

Preaching, teaching, and eldering have been a part of his adult life wherever he has lived. His teachings appeal to college students and church leaders, as well as scholars and laypersons. The church's importance to his life is evident from his beginnings in Thayer. He and his family attended all the Gospel Meetings. He knew all the ministers who preached those meetings, and he was a curious child with a lot of questions. In the community

Introduction

in which he grew up, the church was dominant, prominent, and tightly woven into the fabric of the community. This collection of childhood memories provides the back story on the makings of this exceptional scholar and churchman.

Tom also mentored his students well. Tom tells of being out with his two younger brothers when he was about eight years old. His three-year-old brother followed Tom into an area in which there were a lot of cans and broken glass. His little brother cut his foot badly. Tom says that when his father heard the story " . . . he got his razor strap and hit me across the back of my two legs two or three times. He considered me my brothers' keeper." This brief sketch is one example of a good number of life lessons that Tom learned from his family and friends. He tells of losing an important friend when he was in the second grade because he (Tom) shared a secret that his friend had asked him not to share. He says, "I learned the hard way . . . Being a revealer of secrets is destructive to friendships." He valued good friends and learned from this loss.

Throughout his high school years Tom lived with his uncle and aunt (Cleo and Ova Taylor, our mutual relatives through marriage) in Alton, Missouri. He speaks warmly of those years, especially about how much he learned from Cleo. He talks about Cleo as a mentor to him. His uncle was a high school agriculture teacher and owned a large ranch. During Tom's time with his aunt and uncle, he and his uncle heard about World War II on the radio. They milked cows before school, and Tom "slopped" pigs after school and did other chores. They built fences and worked with Angora goats and horses, and Cleo owned the first pick-up hay bailer in Oregon County. Tom refers to these years as "great boot camp years for life ahead." Among the things he says he learned from Cleo were discipline, how to manage time, the value of knowledge and education, and coping with the world "heads up."

As my mentor and graduate advisor at ACU, Tom suggested that I do my thesis on a female German liberationist theologian, Dorothee Soelle. In retrospect, that was a bold suggestion to make in the mid-to-late 1970s, in a Church of Christ school. Liberation Theology was not a part of the curriculum. However, it was a good suggestion for me. I have never asked him why he suggested her. I suspect he thought her writing was cutting edge and that she would keep my attention. She did. There were no exceptions with the political theologians of that era.

After I left Abilene I discovered another benefit of having Tom Olbricht as my advisor—he had basically signed on to be my advisor for life.

Introduction

He never told me that—not in words anyway. To have an academic advisor for life is a special gift. And Tom did not do this just for me. I am confident that he made himself accessible to all his students. I say this because all of us (hundreds of us) seem to stay in touch with him, or perhaps I should say he stays in touch with us! He took his dad's statement—to be his "brothers' keeper"—to heart. He has been there to assist with finishing theses, career choices, coping with church-related issues, and working to open career opportunities for us. On a personal level, he is a man who knows a lot about the art of friendship keeping. I suspect that is the real value of what he learned from the friend he lost in childhood.

Tom concludes his memoir by pointing to the confidence he acquired in college, saying "I had taken my boot training in the Ozarks and I was adequately prepared to face the future whatever its course."

One of the treasures of these collected memories is the clarity of his recall and the vast number of detailed and unembellished memories of his everyday life in a small community. Even if a reader does not know Tom Olbricht, this collection makes an excellent addition to Ozarks Studies because of the stories lived out in the Thayer community. This book also holds value for those who want to probe more deeply into what is meant by the popular phrase "It takes a village." Tom's memoirs have much to say about lived religion and faith. He speaks to the importance of extended family and a united community in the nurturing of its youngest members. It was a life that ebbed and flowed. Tom's young romances brought frustrations, but they were tolerated. World War II was real, and his family was not isolated from its effects; however, even the war was taken in stride. The importance of education shows up in every chapter—either directly or indirectly. It seemed to be the main contributor to his own family's ability to sustain a good life.

In 2011, Tom was awarded an honorary doctorate at Pepperdine University. Professor Carl Holladay, of Emory University, closed his tribute to Tom with these descriptive words: "child of the church, teacher of the church, servant of the church, and scholar extraordinaire, . . ." With this volume, readers can know and appreciate the deep childhood roots of that child, teacher, and servant.

Kathy J. Pulley
Professor of Religious Studies
Missouri State University
Springfield, MO

Chapter I

Memories Embellished?

I was born in Thayer, Missouri, in 1929. I left my Missouri home to enter Harding University as a freshman in the fall of 1947. Since that time I have only returned to visit. But Missouri remains deeply entrenched in my very psyche via indelible memories. "Precious memories, how they linger, how they ever flood my soul," in the words of the old Gospel song.

I recall late March days, deep blue skies and balmy uplift breezes rustling in the trees. It was great weather for kite flying which I dearly loved. After watching the kite soar aloft on a perfect flying day I lay in the newly blossomed clover with my brothers relishing the warmth and the sweet clover smell. We watched the bees buzz from bloom to bloom. It always seemed a shame to wind up the ball of string in order to go to supper, though we always welcomed a chance to eat.

I also loved the late days of August as the fields dried up. We played in the dusk as the shadows cast long images across the front yard. The cares of the day were past. We played hide and seek, kick the can or similar games. The air was still warm. Sometimes with my uncle we sought out a swimming hole on Warm Fork Creek. The cooler water began to modify the heat at eye level. Most of our swimming holes were surrounded by native sycamores adding a special aroma to the air. I have traveled to Buenos Aries, Lake Louise, Auckland, Nairobi and Beijing, but I have never elsewhere experienced that exact relaxing smell.

I loved walking through the woods on a foggy night in November with my uncle and others as we listened to the baying of our Bluetick "coon hound." We were surrounded by a damp chill, but our jackets and walking kept us warm. On our caps we wore carbide miner's lamps so as to navigate through the trees and underbrush. Sometimes the hound picked up a 'possum' trail rather than that of a raccoon. We weren't too interested in possums because coon hides brought about $20 whereas a possum hide at best was $5. We therefore called off the dog when we thought he was on the trail of a possum. In those days neither raccoons nor possums were plentiful because they were constantly hunted for whatever little money their pelts brought.

I loved early spring when woodland grasses had turned brown as well as the fallen leaves and those that remained on the trees. Many farmers burned leaves in order, so they thought, for the grass to get a head start. An acrid, smoky smell filled the cool night air. My uncle, Cleo Taylor, was a Vocational Agriculture Teacher. At that time the studies suggested that burning impeded rather than helped the grass along. My uncle had a thousand acres of woodlands brush and grass. Contiguous neighbors burned their fields and especially if the wind accelerated the fire lines threatened our fields. We were determined to stop the flames from crossing our fence line. We jumped in the pickup taking along hoes, shovels, rakes and pitchforks in order to impede the advance of the flames. Sometimes we set back fires if the wind was right and worked to keep the fires out. It was hard, sweaty, soot-faced work. We often stayed out until one or two A.M. But I loved being out with the sights and smells. I relished the fact that we often were able to impede and contain the soaring flames.

My memory of southern Missouri was that the optimum time of the year weather-wise was the middle of June. The grass was luxurious, the nights cool and day time temperatures mild. A number of field and forest flowers were in bloom giving off pleasant smells. The birds sang all the day long in the words of a Tin-pan Alley tune. By time I was forty I had lived in Illinois, Iowa, Massachusetts, Pennsylvania and Texas. I never experienced a time in these states comparable to June in Missouri. Since in those years I was either going to graduate school or teaching, June was never a convenient time for a visit back home. As the time passed by I got to thinking that perhaps my love of a Missouri June was the figment of a boyhood imagination. I decided it couldn't be as good as I recalled. But then one year it became possible to visit my home region in June. I just couldn't believe how the weather and place were almost exactly as I remembered. Both my love for a Missouri June and my boyhood memories were fully vindicated.

Memories Embellished?

I remembered Missouri especially because of warm relationships experienced in an extended family of grandparents, uncles and aunts and cousins galore. We often visited our relatives in town and on farms. Sometimes I stayed overnight with cousins. We played, fished and worked in gardens. Our more immediate family always gathered on holidays and on Sundays after church. We played football and softball. We sometimes checked out the cattle and goats. The woods were full of all sorts of relatives several with whom we had little contact. But we and they knew who we were. We had our place in the sun and in the community. We clearly identified with the time and place. These memories had few glitches that cast a dark spell over the realities. Missouri was a place of fulfillment and contentment as I reflect back upon the halcyon days of my youth.

My Missouri heritage has served me well. When asked I have always been pleased to announce that I spent my first, almost eighteen years in Missouri (1929–1947). I grew up on the Arkansas border so that I often made short trips into that state but spent less than a week overnight there. Otherwise my early years were spent in Missouri. I did not visit another state until well into my eighteenth year. In June 1948 I traveled to DeKalb, Illinois, to work for the summer canning peas and corn for the California Packing Company and detasseling corn for the DeKalb Agriculture Association. While there I also ventured into Wisconsin. I have fond memories of growing up in Missouri. I learned much from relatives, teachers and friends that has served me well in life. I have always appreciated my past even though I have made every effort to live in the present. I have relished reliving these events as I recounted the memories of that time and place.

I was born in the house of my parents a hundred yards south of the Thayer, Missouri, city limits. Thayer did not have a hospital and most babies were born at home. Dr. Barnes was called when it was apparent the time drew near. Women relatives may have been present in the house, but Barnes requested that the father absent himself. I was the second child of my parents, my sister Nedra being fourteen months older. The circumstances as to why I was born in Missouri are unusual.

WHY I WAS BORN IN MISSOURI

I was born in Missouri on my mother's side because of a failed mortgage and on my father's side because of a major snow storm. Since my mother's forbears came to Missouri a half century before my father's I will recount the story of the failed mortgage first.

A Failed Mortgage

My great-grandparents John Moody Taylor (1829–1909) and Amy AnthumWaits Taylor (1837–1901) came to Oregon County in 1869 from Franklin County, Alabama. Altogether they had thirteen children and by 1919 sixty-eight grandchildren. Most of their descendents into the second generation were members of the Churches of Christ, and many into the sixth plus generation.[1]

John Moody may have been born in Franklin County, Tennessee, or perhaps Mississippi. Before the Civil War he moved to Alabama. Traditions held that his father, John Taylor, was born either in Northern Ireland or Indiana. My grandfather, Thomas Shelton Taylor, always called himself an Irishman. In 1854 John Moody and Amy Anthum Waits were married in northwest Alabama. She was born in Muscle Shoals, Alabama, in 1837. Her parents were Simeon C. Waits (1803–1880), born in Franklin County, Alabama and Judah (Judy) Hester Waits (1814–1899), born in Person County, North Carolina. It is likely that John Moody Taylor and Amy Anthum Waits were baptized and became members of the Churches of Christ at the same time, perhaps a few years after they were married in 1854. A Restorationist preacher by the name of John Taylor who as far as I can discover was not related baptized John and Amy. John Taylor was influenced by Tolbert Fanning (1810–1874) the latter who in turn was influenced by Alexander Campbell. Fanning was a Nashville preacher who spent considerable time evangelizing in northern Alabama. My grandfather, T. Shelt Taylor, reported that the Taylors heard the famous Churches of Christ evangelist, T. B. Larimore (1843–1929) preach meeting sermons. Larimore evangelized in various places in Northern Alabama in 1868 with John Taylor.[2] John and Amy Taylor left Alabama for southern Missouri the next year in 1869.

Three sisters of Amy Anthum Waits Taylor, the mother of my grandfather Taylor, were the first of my ancestors to move to Oregon Country from Franklin Country Alabama. One married M. George Norman, who became

---

1. This information is taken from genealogical information compiled by Mary Ann Taylor Talley, my third cousin and my mother's brother Wellington Thomas Taylor. Tom, as he was called later in life, was the youngest of the sixty-eight grandchildren.

2. Srygley, *Biographies and Sermons*, 95.

a judge, and the other Jesse Morris, who owned a major lumberyard. They came to Oregon County about 1849 from Alabama.[3] Another sister, Martha Ann Waits, married Richard Livingston Langley, born in Franklin County Alabama. A brother of Amy Anthum Waits Taylor, Simon C. Waits, Sr., later also came to Missouri. To my knowledge those who moved to Missouri before the Civil War were not Restorationists but mostly Baptists.

My great grandfather Taylor, John Moody Taylor, was an Alabama confederate soldier in the Civil War. Before the war he had been a slave overseer for a wealthy widow who owned a plantation. He was known as a compassionate manager who fed and treated his subordinates well.

After the war John Moody Taylor farmed near Belgreen, in northwestern Alabama. In the 1960s my Uncle Tom Taylor became interested in family genealogy. One day while visiting with his father T. Shelt Taylor, Tom mentioned that he and his wife Dortha planned a trip to northern Alabama to look into certain details regarding the family history. My grandfather became patently agitated and told my uncle that under no circumstances was he to take this trip. He informed Uncle Tom that he needed to know something about the reason his parents left Alabama that had not been reported to Tom and his siblings.

Grandpa related this story. In the early days of reconstruction John Moody's brother Thomas bought a farm for which John Moody also signed the note. After a few years it became clear to Thomas that he would be unable to make enough money to meet the mortgage payments. After the note

---

3. Maj. M. G. Norman was born in Tennessee in 1829. He went to Oregon, County, Missouri, as a pioneer of 1849. He was engaged in farming, but was also a member of the legal profession and a man well educated and well informed as to important events and affairs. Just after the days of the Reconstruction period, he was sent as the first representative from Oregon County to the Missouri State Legislature for two terms. He did not again fill public office, but remained as a prominent and active democrat during the remainder of his life and was considered one of the strong and influential men of his party in Oregon County. He passed away there in 1907, aged seventy-eight years. As a farmer, Mr. Norman made a success of his ventures and always bore an excellent reputation in business circles. During the Civil war he enlisted in a Missouri regiment in the Confederate service, was elected to captain of his company, and through brave and faithful service was advanced to the rank of major, serving under Generals Price and Marmaduke. He was a deacon in the Baptist Church and was fraternally affiliated with the lodges of the Masons and the Odd Fellows orders. Mr. Norman married Miss Mary Ann Waits, who was born in 1830, in Alabama, and died in Oregon County, Missouri, in 1910, and they became the parents of seven children. This information was taken from an on-line webpage regarding James C. Norman, a son, who moved to Oklahoma and became a judge.

holders pressed Thomas, he disappeared, perhaps first to Texas and then on to California. He was never heard of again. John Moody had little money either, and much of the white population at that time was migrating west from Alabama. Since his wife's sisters had moved to Missouri, John and his family pulled up stakes in 1869 and settled in Oregon County around Couch. The precipitating event of the unpaid mortgage therefore became a critical reason why my mother's grandparents migrated by covered wagon to southern Missouri and northern Arkansas. My grandfather T. Shelt Taylor was afraid that if my uncle nosed around too much there might be repercussions from the failure to pay off the century-old mortgage.

A Major Snow Storm

My father's parents moved to Missouri because of Nebraska snow storms. In 1910 my German-born grandfather Henry Olbricht (1856–1941) decided that he did not care for the blizzards that swept across Western Nebraska. He was born in what was then Glatz, Silesia, Germany (now Klodzko, Poland), and migrated to the United States in 1878. He was nominally Roman Catholic, which he remained until his death. His first wife, my grandmother Katherine Eick, was born in Regensberg, Germany. They both lived in Elizabeth, New Jersey, when they met. She died in 1889. My grandfather remarried a widow, Bertha Lange Sauser, in 1900, a sister of his brother Joseph's wife. She was born in a German-speaking village that was variously in Poland or Russia and was Lutheran. After living in Nebraska for 18 years my grandfather started looking for a warmer climate and knew a man who had moved from Nebraska to Missouri. In scrutinizing real estate ads Grandpa Henry was attracted by the description of a farm near Mountain Grove, Missouri. He and my step-grandmother took a train from Crawford, Nebraska, visited the farm, and left a down payment. They next decided to visit the man they had known in Nebraska. This man owned two farms east of Thayer, Missouri, and told my grandfather he would sell him either. My grandfather decided he liked the farm situated at the headwaters of Janes Creek better than the one in Mountain Grove so he made arrangements to buy it.

A remarkable story passed on in the family relates the details of the blizzard that triggered my grandfather's determination to move from Nebraska to a more temperate climate. One day my grandfather hitched up his team and traveled about ten miles northeast of the ranch to Glen, Nebraska, at which was located the closest post office. As he turned around and headed home he was caught in a terrible blizzard with temperatures in the teens and wind blasts of thirty miles an hour. Snow depths reached upwards from twenty inches. Meanwhile back at the ranch my grandmother and the children waited anxiously for his return. My father was in his middle twenties. Sometime in the late afternoon the horses returned with evidence that they had been released from the wagon. The family was deeply concerned, but decided they couldn't do anything until morning. Soon after daybreak my father and Uncle Ernest Sauser, my step-grandmother's son, saddled their horses and started on the trail to Glen. After traveling a few miles they saw the wheels of the upside down wagon rising above the fallen snow. With fearful anticipation they hurried to the wagon and turned it over. They discovered grandfather asleep and no worse for the night in the chill. It was fortunate that he was a tanner by profession for which he had apprenticed in Germany. He had various hides on the wagon and some with heavy fur. He had released the horses then wrapped up in the furs and turned the wagon over on top of himself

Grandfather Olbricht sold his Nebraska land to my father. My father raised potatoes in Nebraska and took them by train to southern Missouri to sell them while at the same time visiting his parents. My grandfather T. Shelt Taylor ran a gas station/small grocery and bought produce in season in truck load lots. In the course of selling potatoes my father made arrangement with my mother's father, T. Shelt, to sell potatoes at his place. My grandfather was impressed with my father and thought he should meet his "old maid schoolteacher" daughter who was teaching away from Thayer at some distance. A meeting was arranged, and a mutual interest developed. In April 1927 my parents (age 41 and 29) were married and spent the next three months touring in Wyoming and Idaho and doing summer ranch work on the Nebraska homestead. My mother, however, was not too pleased with western Nebraska, so they decided to settle in southern Missouri, which they did that fall. I turned out to be a Missourian as the result of a failed mortgage and a ferocious blizzard.[4]

---

4. I have published two autobiographies which provide much detail about my life after I left Missouri in 1947. Olbricht, *Hearing God's Voice,* and Olbricht, *Reflections on My Life.*

Chapter II
———

A Depression Child

On October 28, 1929, "Black Monday," the Dow lost 13% of its value. The next day, Tuesday, October 29, 1929, "Black Tuesday," the stock market in high volume sales lost another 12%. On that day certain banks closed their doors. The great "crash" had arrived! I was born five days later, November 3, 1929, "Black Sunday." I used to tell my college students that my parents had two crashes in succession, five days apart, the banks closed and then I appeared. The doctor made house calls, and I was born in our residence, two hundred yards south of the Thayer, Missouri, city limits and one mile north of the Missouri-Arkansas state line. Dr. Barnes did not appreciate husbands being in his way so he sometimes suggested that husbands go fishing. I don't know where my father went, perhaps to the barn, but I never knew my father to fish, though he had as a younger man in Nebraska.

My father, Benjamin Joseph Olbricht (1885–1978) turned 44, November 10, 1929, a week after I was born. My mother, Agnes Taylor Olbricht, was 31. My father was born in Elizabeth, New Jersey, to German immigrant parents. His mother died when he was four. Two years later his father, Henry Olbricht, homesteaded in Sioux County, Western Nebraska, where his cousin Robert Bittner preceded him. Henry remarried in 1900. My mother and father married in 1927. She was 29 and he 41. They had four children, Nedra in 1928, me in 1929, Glenn in 1931 and Owen in 1932.

My mother was born in North Central Arkansas. In her younger years her parents, T. Shelt and Myrtle Taylor, moved to Thayer, Missouri. When she finished high school in 1916, she started teaching in one room country schools. She taught for a time south of Kansas City in Bates County, then in Thomasville, MO. When she could, mostly in the summers, she took courses at Southwest Missouri State Teacher's College in Springfield (now Missouri State University), receiving a degree in 1924. When she met my father she was perceived by standards of the day as being an "old maid" school teacher. She was introduced to my father by her father T. Shelt Taylor when he visited his parents east of Thayer. My Olbricht grandparents left Nebraska in 1910 because of the blizzards and bought a farm east of Thayer. My father, accompanied by a sizable shipment of his Nebraska potatoes, sold them at my grandfather Taylor's store. My parents married in Thayer and spent their honeymoon in the northwest around Yellowstone, going on to Idaho and returning to the Nebraska homestead. There they cut and stacked hay. In the fall they moved to Thayer, Missouri, to raise their family. Mother said she was homesick for trees, but more likely she was homesick for relatives who filled the woods in our region of the Ozarks.

I, of course, have no memory of the early days of the Great Depression. My earliest memories are of being at an outdoor Gospel Meeting at the Centertown Church of Christ between Thayer, Missouri, and Mammoth Spring, Arkansas, and of the wedding of my Uncle Cleo Taylor in 1934. The meeting took place on the church building lot, under large oak trees with strings of light bulbs overhead and the stars beyond. Uncle Cleo Taylor married Ova Martin at the house of her parents, Jim and Dessie Martin, August 19, 1934. The wedding took place on the wide front steps of their Mammoth Spring native stone house. Mammoth was immediately south of Thayer just a mile over the Arkansas line. The residence was on a hill slope, and the steps to the front door were ten feet across, about twelve steps in all up from the main street. With the minister at the top center, the bride and groom and the attendants occupied various step levels down in suits and colorful gowns.

THE IMPACT OF THE DEPRESSION

The Depression didn't impact my family as it did some. My father had made considerable money growing potatoes in Nebraska during and after World War I. For a time, before he met my mother, he considered retiring and moving to Florida. A growing family after he married, however, dictated that he settle in and work in various forms of construction, often building houses and barns with one of mother's cousins, Rob Hicks. Rob lived on a small farm about 6 miles southeast of Mammoth Spring. He was a nephew of my grandmother, Myrtle Taylor, and his wife a niece of my grandfather, T. Shelt Taylor. Rob and my father built houses for various relatives and others. Rob was a finishing carpenter with a wood working shop on his farm, and along with constructing houses, built furniture especially out of wild cherry which grew in abundance throughout the region. My father helped in whatever way needed, mixing mortar for laying native stones or constructing the house framework. He specialized in finishing oak floors and painting the houses. He also worked some for my grandfather, when needed, at his gas station/grocery store. Both he and my mother had saved money and he had additional income from leasing out the Nebraska ranch. To my knowledge my father never borrowed any money after he paid off the land in Nebraska that he purchased from my grandparents.

We grew much of what we ate on our eleven acres. We had about two acres of wheat which dad took to the local mill for grinding. Mom used the whole grain flour for baking bread and which the rest the family ate as a hot breakfast cereal much like Ralston, a commercial cereal product. He also had a small heavy duty hand grinder and ground some himself in small amounts. Mom thought the healthiest bread was made from whole ground grain which she called graham bread. The whole family loved it. We had plenty of hickory and walnuts on the farm as well as persimmons that grew wild. Blackberries were readily available on our farm, at my grandfather's and elsewhere. In areas near my Olbricht grandparents' farm we could pick huckleberries and, on their farm, wild plums. We had a large orchard with apples, pears, plums, grapes, cherries, gooseberries, raspberries, strawberries and especially peaches. For vegetables we grew both white and sweet potatoes, onions, carrots, beets, parsnips, turnips, kohlrabies, spinach of various kinds, kale, leaf lettuce, cucumbers, green beans, black eyed and cow peas, Swiss chard, cabbage, radishes, tomatoes, okra, squash, asparagus, rhubarb, and even peanuts. I don't recall growing sweet corn. I don't think my father, good German that he was, cared for it. We always had at least one cow for milk, cottage cheese, cream and butter. We had a separator for the cream and churned butter in a gallon hand-turned churn. I recall turning the churn handle myself when I was perhaps five. We had laying hens to produce eggs, and raised fryers, that is, young three to four pound chickens that, at that time, were mostly prepared by frying. Older chickens were boiled with dumplings. We often had a hog or two for pork.

We seldom raised beef to eat. It was one of the few items we bought at a market. We knew the economy was depressed, but my father spent little of his money so we lived in about the same manner of those with far less.

In the middle thirties, Missouri required a poll tax of $2 a year should one wish to vote. The tax finally ended in state elections in 1966 because of a Supreme Court decision. One could fulfill the requirement, not by paying money, but by working on county roads for two days. I was always surprised that my father worked rather than pay the tax. To my knowledge everyone else in my extended family paid the tax. He never minded working, however, and I think he enjoyed getting out in the country and seeing where roads were being built or improved. Even though he had some suspicion of banks because of bank failures during the depression, he maintained a bank account. He invested most of his excess funds in government bonds and insurance. He saved money in this manner all the way through the depression. He read a weekly newspaper, the *Kansas City Grit*, and loved the political criticism of Will Rogers.

THE LESS FORTUNATE

Though my mother had little in excess for assisting others, she was always concerned to do what she could to help the less fortunate. This grew in part from her religious commitments. She was especially influenced by Charles Sheldon's book, *In His Steps* (published in 1896), along with various novels of Lloyd C. Douglas, especially *Magnificent Obsession*. These authors emphasized the importance of addressing the needs of people in towns and communities. Sheldon created the slogan, "What would Jesus do?" and concluded that Jesus looked after the poor. I recall that we had a frame for quilting in my sister's bedroom. The women of the church made quilts for each other—especially to give to the needy. Another project of the Churches of Christ women of our region was to make dresses and shirts out of flower and feed sacks manufactured especially for that purpose. Several different prints were available as well as solids, the former utilized for dresses and the latter for shirts. My grandfather sometimes had extra sacks from feeding ground grains to his cattle. My mother made clothes to give to the needy and dresses for my sister and herself and shirts for us boys from sack material.

I recall us walking about a mile once to take a quilt and a couple of dresses to Mrs. Dawson, wife of Monroe, who was an area drunk. The

Dawsons lived along a gravel road just north of the Arkansas line. Mrs. Dawson sometimes attended services at the Mammoth Spring Church of Christ. They had three children, as I recall. The second, Gerald, was in my class at school and was a rowdy. He was always getting in trouble and being sent to the principal's office. The principals at that time administered spankings with a wooden paddle or a large rubber hose about two feet in length. Gerald received his share. He usually came to school with clean clothes, even if patched, but he soon had them soiled. He loved to play marbles for keeps; that is, all the marbles he hit out of the ring became his. Because of the insistence of our parents, a number of us boys had qualms about playing marbles for keeps, but not Gerald. Each classroom in our elementary school had a cloakroom for coats, boots, and supplies. One form of punishment was sending a rascal to the cloakroom for an hour. One memorable day Gerald was sent to the cloak room. He had his pockets full of marbles. Soon we heard him rolling around on the floor and marbles crashing into the walls. The noises disturbed the class. The teacher opened the door, grabbed Gerald by the back of his shirt collar, and marched him down to the principal's office. I didn't care to be around Gerald, but I knew of his circumstances, so I befriended him when I could. But he did not seek out friendships. I heard that Gerald, in his later high school years, was found dead by the railroad tracks. Very likely he was drunk and a train hit him.

One feature of the Depression years was traveling unemployed itinerants. They rode the rails, that is, in the boxcars, and walked the highways, often hitch hiking. One could frequently see these hoboes, or bums as they were called, in camps along the rail lines at Frisco Springs in Thayer near the Roundhouse. They stayed out of the towns because the officials demanded that they move on. They seemed to multiply when major floods inundated the Mississippi River. Our house was on US 63, a major highway. Often bums walked past our house. My father generally did not have a high regard for bums. If he was home he told them to move along. They usually came to the house, knocked on the door, and asked to work for food. My dad never invited them to do any work because he said they never did it properly. My mother, when he was away at work, however, gave them food, especially in the summer when we had garden products or fruit. She always had whole wheat bread baked and made sandwiches usually of butter and jelly. We made our own jelly and always had plenty, or perhaps offered them bologna we bought in two pound hunks and sliced at home fromgranddad's store. We always had brown bags we bought from my grandfather and wax paper. Mom wrapped the sandwiches in the waxed paper and added them to the bag after first putting a couple of apples or peaches in the bottom. On one occasion, after eating part of his meal, the bum returned to the house, knocked on the door, and told my mother that she gave him too much. She should save some for the next bum who came along. We were the givers not the takers, but we lived much like those receiving help. These were depressed times, and many of these itinerants could not find employment. We saw few hobos after World War II commenced, since jobs multiplied.

My grandparents on both sides were frugal, nevertheless had the means to purchase whatever they desired. Granddad Taylor tended to trade for a new Ford car each year in the 1930s. I recall that in 1937 a new Ford sedan cost about $600 and up depending on what accessories were requested. Grandfather normally bought the basic model except that he liked to listen to the radio so he usually bought one with a radio installed. Uncle Ted Olbricht attended a technical school in Kansas City focusing upon farm equipment. He bought whatever items he thought cost effective including an electric welder which few people owned at that time.

My father was more penny-pinching than most of our relatives, meaning that we were perceived as the poorest in our larger kinship circle. One good example was our telephone arrangement. My mother loved using the telephone, but my father didn't really care to talk on it; he didn't want to pay a phone bill, however inexpensive. He therefore bought two hand-rung wall phones powered by batteries and put one in our house and the other in grandpa Taylor's bedroom. He ran a non-insulated wire on the electrical poles from our house to grandpa's, a half mile away. My mom could talk to grandma, but to no one else. If she wanted to get a message to another person, she called grandma, who wrote it down then called that person on her personal telephone. Grandma also took messages for my mother. Because the wire was non-insulated the phone was useless during an electrical storm. But Dad never had to pay a phone bill! The adult relatives knew that my father had money so they never tried to help us. Perhaps for that reason, however, they gave my siblings and me several gifts. Through the Depression years, we lived like a financially strapped family, but we weren't restrained by the Depression. Our resources gave us a sense of security others didn't have.

Missouri Memories, 1934–1947

MY FATHER

The earliest memories I have of my father is him carrying me to the car when I fell asleep during the sermon after the outdoor Gospel Meeting concluded at the Centertown Church of Christ. He was more manly than gentle. In my early years our two-bedroom house was heated with a large potbellied stove in the fairly large dining room which was in the center of the house. We washed up when we got dirty during the week, or we went swimming in our irrigation tank, but we always took a bath on Saturday night in a thirty-gallon galvanized circular tub, which was about three feet in diameter and a foot and a half deep. In the winter, the tub was set near the stove so we would be warm bathing. For some reason, my father occasionally talked about being ruptured. Rupture was rather common problem with men who did heavy lifting in farm and construction work. As he would dry me off with a towel he would push his finger into my lower abdomen and state that I might be ruptured. That was his way of being playful such as someone poking a child's shoulder and declaring the child had a garment on their back. That scared me because though I didn't understand what being ruptured was all about, I was sure it was to be avoided at all costs.

Dad constructed a "sleeping porch" for Glenn, Owen, and me on top of our cellar, which was an east extension to the house. The cellar, about ten feet lower than the house, had shelves and served as a storage place for all our garden and orchard canned goods put up in glass jars. Part of the room had a dirt floor which served as a root (meaning any vegetable that the part eaten grows beneath the top of the soil) cellar for potatoes, carrots, and parsnips. The screened in back porch separated the "sleeping porch" from the rest of the house. We had two double beds on the sleeping porch. This large room was enclosed with windows that we shut in the winter, but no source of heat was provided. When it got down to zero, which didn't happen too often, it was cold; but my mother had an almost limitless supply of homemade quilts. When we first went to bed my mother would heat water on the wood stove, put it into quart or half gallon jars, wrap the bottle in a towel, and place it in bed at our feet. The glass hot water bottle was a great assist in quickly warming up a cold bed. The bottles had to be removed in the night after they cooled.

Nedra, our sister, slept in one of the beds, and Glenn and I in the other until she got too old at about 7. She then slept in the second bedroom in the house. In my earliest memories the west bedroom was my father's and my mother slept in the other bedroom—first with Glenn, then Owen, our youngest brother, until he reached 3. My father's bedroom was unusual. On the wall he had several hides including a wolf, a coyote, and an antelope, tanned by my grandfather who apprenticed in Germany as a tanner. On the floor was a rug made out of a bear skin with the head still attached. Later the hides collected moths, developed holes, and my mother made him dispose of them.

My father was old enough to be my grandfather. He was not cuddly and seldom touched us. He never played with us. But at night after the work of the day was done, he sat for an hour in a two-seated swing he made which was attached to a large box elder tree fifteen feet away from the house toward the highway and watched the cars go by. He also looked after us and refereed any arguments we got into over rules for hide and seek, tag or other games we played. Mother stayed inside, often reading or doing the dishes and cleaning the house.

Dad involved us in several outside projects. As early as I can recall he had us opening the two field gates at night when he returned from work so he could park the car in the garage. We burned wood for fuel, and since I was somewhat large for my age I brought wood from a stack about a hundred feet from the house in my Red Ryder Wagon to the six steps that led to the back door. I carried the sticks a few at a time and stacked them on the back porch. My brothers helped me when they got old enough. One time after Uncle Cleo bought the Price place south of granddad's he hired some men to cut down the numerous small oak trees that were just the right size for firewood. The wood cutters had a circular saw on a frame with a pulley which could be attached by a belt to a rear jacked-up wheel of their Model A pickup. Pole-size logs were placed on the metal frame and pushed into the circular saw, enabling a rapid cutting of the poles into stove-size lengths. These buzz saws, as we called them, were common in the region. Uncle Cleo told dad that he could have all the wood he wanted. Dad borrowed Grandpa's pickup to haul the wood to our house about a mile away. He took me along to help load. At that time there was considerable fear of black widow spiders. People sometimes died as the result of a bite. One day I had two or three small pieces of wood under my arm carrying them to the pickup when I felt a sting on the inside of my left arm near my arm pit. I cried out and dropped the wood. My dad looked at my arm and saw where I had been bitten. He and others looked around thinking it was a spider, but couldn't locate it. A black widow has a noticeable red spot on its abdomen. My dad cut my arm at that place so it would bleed in case there was poison in my arm. The bite swelled some, and when we got home mom put iodine on it. The next day it still hurt but there were no further complications. It probably wasn't a black widow.

When I was in first grade at Thayer Elementary in the fall of 1935, my father and mother's cousin, Rob Hicks, were involved in building a nice stone house for Uncle Norval three blocks south of the school. Uncle Norval had a good paying job with a secure future as the Standard Oil bulk agent for Oregon Country. He delivered gas, oil, and supplies to all the Standard Oil stations in the county as well as to some large farms. I had to pass the building site on the way to and from school. The house was to have a basement. A man with a large work horse that dragged a scoop removed much of the dirt. I doubt if there were any private bulldozers in our region. Some blasting had to be done to break up hardpan soil and rocks and the rest shoveled out by hand. Foundations were first poured using a small cement mixer. The cement was conveyed to the proper location by running wheelbarrows down a ramp. Next, the walls of the basement were poured then the frame was erected. All the wood employed was oak since that was what grew in our region and therefore the least expensive. Some of the oak was green and therefore easier into which to drive nails. Some, however, was seasoned because otherwise the green boards would shrink resulting in cracks in walls. Seasoned oak is extremely hard, and driving nails into it is exceptionally difficult. Sometimes the nails bounce and other times they bend. If they bent, the carpenter pulled them out and dropped them on the ground or on the subfloor. In those days an effort was made to save everything possible because money was scarce. It was my job to go around the site, pick up all the nails, and put them in a gallon bucket. If they were bent one of the workmen would straighten them for later use. I always liked to be a part of the adult activities so I welcomed the opportunity. I only lost interest when the work became routine, for example, nightly hauling in of firewood.

I recall another project on which I felt privileged to work. We had a windmill on our well that provided all the needed water for the house, the animals, and the garden plots when there was adequate wind. We also had an electric pump we could use if we did not have enough wind to keep the storage tank full. But Dad wanted to pay as little for electricity as possible. Since our property was low on a hill sloping to the east, Dad decided that if we elevated the windmill the increased wind would provide adequate additional water. The tower was about 30 feet. Of course it was possible to purchase a taller tower, but that cost money. My dad's solution was to place 4, 16 foot 4 X 4s in the well house, tear down the old tower then re-erect it on top of the 4 X 4s. Though I was only seven, my dad wanted me to help out by letting down and handing up parts with a block and tackle. For the main work he hired another man to help him, perhaps a couple of days. Dad had erected windmills on his ranch in Nebraska and for other ranchers there. The old windmill was disassembled first and laid out on the ground. The four wooden posts were attached to poured foundations about a foot square and two feet deep in the well house and stabilized with diagonal cross pieces. The tower steel was then attached piece by piece on top of the 4 X 4s until the mill was reassembled. The rotor was pulled to the top with a block and tackle. The blades were pulled up the same way, the "fan" rebuilt, and voila, the mill was ready to operate. I also recall Dad assembling a windmill at Uncle Ernest Sauser's east of Thayer, and I helped a bit with that one too. My father was not much of a companion, but he was good at involving me in what he did whenever he could. Fortunately, however, in our extended family, I had uncles and cousins who were good companions.

My father molded me into a role in which I took the lead and assumed responsibility. My sister Nedra was older, but it was generally assumed that it was I who was responsible for my brothers, not her. When I started first grade at age 5, turning 6 in November, we walked to school about a half mile to the north. My sister was in the second grade, and she was by now accustomed to walking both ways with three or four neighborhood girls. I assumed I would be walking with them since there were no boys my age. It went fine the first week, but the girls soon decided they wanted to walk on their own and not be bothered with a younger brother who had a difficult time keeping up. One day they ran off and left me. I was put out and felt ill treated. I thought I would show them! I just wouldn't go to school that day. I returned home. I soon learned, however, that in a family of teachers one did not skip school—period—unless one came down with the mumps or measles. My mother said that she and my brothers would walk with me half way, but I would have to do the rest on my own. I was certainly displeased with that turn of events, but it was clear I had no alternative. From then on I made my way to school, sometimes with a group, but sometimes on my own. My parents did not insist that my sister wait for me. It was my responsibility to get there.

In 1937, when I was in the second grade, an epidemic of polio hit our region. It especially attacked young boys. My parents and grandparents were concerned. We heard of two or three boys in town who were my age coming down with polio, one of whom was Jack Webber who lived in a house on the street where I walked about half way to school. My mother told me I had to walk an alternate parallel street that was to the west which I could pick up north of our house. I wasn't too happy at first, but then I discovered that three or four of my classmates walked this route, among whom was Bernadine Pingleton, an attractive girl, our classroom favorite. We cut up a bit on the way, and I initiated a few antics to try to impress Bernadine. She at least took notice. After about a year the polio scare died down.

As I walked to school in 1938, a mentally challenged teenage boy who was kept at home—somewhat common at that time—was out in the yard making loud noises. The neighbors all knew about him and gave him little attention. He saw me across the street, yelled incoherent words, and threw rocks large enough to cause damage were I hit. I didn't take this lightly. I could have speeded up and run on toward school, but I decided to scare him off and threw rocks back. I think I hit him with a small one and he went bellowing into his house. His mother came out and noticed me, and I kept going toward school. She called the school and reported that I threw rocks at her son. I admitted as much but told them that this (Hinkle) boy who was twice my size threw at me first. I was surprised that they weren't impressed by my explanation. They told me not to do it again and informed my Aunt Alice who taught home economics at Thayer High. Aunt Alice told my mother, and I was whipped with switches across my legs and told just to stay away from the Hinkle house and never do it again. In another year the Hinkles decided to institutionalize their son.

Dad expected me to look after my two younger brothers—Glenn and Owen. They liked to wrestle and shout at one another far more than I, so one day I decided I would slip away and go play in the ditches in the large field back of our house. Sometimes neighborhood guys my age were playing there. The field had once been farmed, but it was badly eroded with ditches about as deep as I was tall. It was a great place for playing. We molded mud balls to lob at each other like fighting from trenches in WWI. We tried to dig caves into the walls but without much success. If the stream running down through the field was flowing, as it did in the spring, we loved to build dams so as to back the water up for wading, then, when it was time to go home, break the dam and watch the water rush downstream. We had a stile for crossing over into the adjoining pasture, but it wasn't in the best of repair. As I tried to give my brothers the slip, unfortunately, I was seen by one, and they both started following me. They went down to a corner where we collected cans and broken glass. After the rubbish accumulated for a time my father dug a hole and buried it. We always went barefooted in warm weather. Owen, who at that time was 3, probably not knowing any better, walked through the cans and broken glass and cut his foot deeply. He went back to the house crying, and I made my getaway. But when my father got home he got his razor strap and hit me across the back of my legs two or three times. He considered me my brothers' keeper.

MOTHER

Before my mother married she spent most of her life as a teacher, and however good at it, she was dedicated. She was more of a dispenser of insight than a cuddler and affirmer. In my earliest memories we spent at least part of the day with her reading to us. I remember on a warm day in early April, likely 1935, mother decided we should go for a walk in the pasture northeast of the house. She took a book and cookies to nibble on. She found a nice sunny place along the fence, had us sit in a circle in a clover patch, and proceeded to read. She may have brought along poetry by Henry Wadsworth Longfellow or a work by Robert Lewis Stevenson. Normally, after eating our cookies we walked a bit. A copse of oak and persimmon trees of about an acre grew at a higher level a short distance across a little stream east of our property. The trees were perhaps twenty years old and dense, creating a dark interior to the copse. Two or three walking paths ambled through the woods. One time Nedra and I walked there on our own and got lost in the copse. We were quite scared, having read the story of Hansel and Gretel! We heard various noises and ran, finally making our way out of the woods, but on the side away from the house. In another year, however, we were able to navigate our way among the trees and loved to play there, though our parents preferred that we play elsewhere.

My mother, bless her heart, was not fond of washing dishes or doing housework. For some reason she didn't always insist that Nedra help her. When I was seven she developed an assembly line in which I washed the dishes, Glenn, age five, dried, and Owen, age four, put away the silverware, pots and pans, and some of the dishes. While we worked mother read from Hurlbert's Bible Story book. She was an animated reader, and I didn't mind washing. I'm sure we would have preferred being outside playing marbles, tossing a ball around, or exploring in the fields, but mother tried to be enticing so we humored her.

Mother liked us to read, in fact, even at times when Dad thought we should be outside doing chores or playing. He thought that reading led to mental problems—especially reading the Bible. My mother, therefore, read the Bible when he was at work. The Thayer library was down in the business part of town. We had streets to the east that were a shortcut, but it was still more than a mile walk. We normally made a trip to the library once a week. The library would let each of us check out three books. On the way back home, carrying our books, we got tired and complained, telling mom we had to rest. But when we got nearer home we often took off running and left mom behind. I read such books as the Rover Boys or Rebecca of Sunnybrook Farm. But I loved most of all a series of boys' books called Mark Tidd. Mark was an editor and inventor. I especially loved his inventiveness. I had read about Thomas A. Edison and wanted to follow in his footsteps as an inventor. My first two names were Thomas and Henry. I used to tell my friends I was named after Thomas A. Edison and Henry Ford. When they expressed surprise, I would respond, saying, "Well, I wasn't named before them!"

When I was about six, Mother showed signs of mental stress, and commenced acting and talking abnormally. I recall once at Uncle Norval's she walked around barefoot and made off-the-wall comments. I knew my relatives were a bit worried because my grandmother's sister was in a state mental institution at Farmington, Missouri. My relatives weren't clear as to what was to be done, but they thought she was showing symptoms of a nervous breakdown. She had given birth to four children in five years and was nearing 35. Her siblings decided that we children needed to stay with relatives to give mom a chance to rest up. It was determined that Nedra and I should stay with Uncle Norval and Aunt Mabel since they lived close to our school. Glenn and Owen went to stay with Rob and Stella Hicks. Rob was my father's working partner. Stella was a pleasant woman and invited us to spend a night or two with them at other times. I think we four stayed away from home about two weeks, and mother had so improved that she could take us back. My dad was concerned enough about her condition to help more around the house. From then on mom was always interested in food that was supposed to enhance mental heath, especially greens of all sorts and yeast. We walked the roadways in the spring picking wild greens such as dandelions and dock.

A Depression Child

Another memory of my mother is of her going to visit people. My dad's work always took him away from home. We therefore walked wherever we went. It wasn't too bad to walk up to Ruby Powell's, about three blocks west. Ruby was a member of the Church of Christ, and she and my mother talked about church matters. Ruby had a daughter Nadine with whom Nedra, my sister, played and a son Billy, with whom I played some. But we were never as close as Nedra and Nadine. Another visit I recall which happened when I was about five was to the small house of Luther Havens, a twin of my great-grandmother Lucy Dunsmore, born in Ionia, Michigan. Luther, at a young age, moved from Michigan to South Dakota and raised a family. He and my great-grandmother had not seen each other for perhaps sixty years, but when his wife died he moved to Thayer, MO in 1932. Luther died two years later. Not long after his death, I recall going to visit his daughter, Lavina, and another woman. I'm not sure who the other woman was. They lived about a quarter mile southwest along a small stream that ran through Greentown in a small frame house with two bedrooms. The Havens were descended from a Lady-in-Waiting to Queen Mary (1516–1558) of England. I recall them talking about British royalty. I didn't know until later that Ladies-in-Waiting were normally of the royal family.

Often my mother went to visit persons because they had come to our house offering religious instruction. She frequently paid them a return visit. One of the women was a Jehovah's Witness. We walked about a mile to get to her house. When we arrived she set up a small record player, likely a 78, and played a miniature record of a Jehovah Witness professor teaching some item of their doctrine. The woman and my mother talked at length, but neither made much headway in persuading the other. A Reorganized Church of Jesus Christ of the Latter Day Saints (Independence, MO, now designated Community of Christ) was located a quarter of a mile from our house near the town park. I recall going there to talk with a woman from that church. My mother not only liked to read, but to write. She wrote short articles for *Christian Woman* published in Wichita, Kansas. She also wrote letters, mostly to relatives, and would generally do so at night when the rest of us were asleep. As a teacher she wrote in a somewhat large cursive style and her hand writing was always easy to read.

One of my mother's concerns was that our father might become a Christian. He was raised a Roman Catholic in Nebraska, but his father didn't often attend Mass since the distance was so great. Dad had various views that certain Catholics held, one of which was that only priests could understand the Scripture. Nevertheless, as early as I can remember he attended church with us. The conviction in Churches of Christ was that becoming a Christian entails believer's baptism by immersion, and Roman Catholics practice infant sprinkling. Finally in 1938, when I was 8, my father was baptized in the Spring River below the dam at Mammoth Spring. I'm sure my mother was the main catalyst, but Dad had learned to appreciate the preachers. What impressed me at the time of his baptism was that he became kinder than I had ever seen him. Before, he was focused on getting the job done with little time for small niceties. He was strict in regard to us completing our chores, but not harsh. Now he was kind and considerate and gave more thought to how he could help people. At first I thought, "Can this be my Dad?" but I became accustomed to his change in attitude. No one was more pleased than my mother.

Chapter III

Ozark Christmas in 1936[1]

Christmas was by far my favorite time of the year the winter of 1936 when I was seven. The second Sunday in December the parents of my cousin James Ray Dunsmore invited me to go with them for lunch following church at his Martin grandparents, and afterward we would cut Christmas trees. That was the best proposal I had heard for some time. It signaled that Christmas was finally on the way.

My cousin James Ray Dunsmore and I at that age and in southern Missouri were called by our first two names, mine being Thomas Henry. We were given the first names of our maternal and paternal grandfathers, Jim Martin and Ray Dunsmore and Thomas Shelton Taylor and Henry Olbricht.

To cut the trees we had to drive out to one of the Martin farms in the country ten miles southwest of Mammoth Spring, Arkansas. James Ray and I hurried through the meal, and after the adult talk wound down my Uncle Cleo, who was also at the lunch with his wife Ova, suggested that it was time to go. Cleo, my mother's brother, married Ova Martin a sister to James Ray's mother—Opal Martin Dunsmore. James Ray's father, Bynum, was a Barber in Thayer, Missouri, and a double cousin to Cleo Taylor and my mother. That means that Cleo and Bynam's parents married brothers and sisters.

---

1. Chapter II is slightly revised from, Olbricht, "Recalling Ozarks Past: Winter 1936," 12–25.

Missouri Memories, 1934–1947

James Ray and I headed out the back door, jumped on the running board of the 1936 Ford pickup, and climbed into the back. It was a sunny day but Cirrus clouds—mare-tails as we called them—stretched across the sky. The temperature was in the sixties and a bit on the cool side, but we wore jackets. As Uncle Cleo turned onto the street James Ray and I huddled behind the cab. It served as a windbreaker and a dust shield as we headed down a graveled country road. Along the way we viewed farmhouses, cows and horses, goats, and flocks of crows.

After twenty minutes my Uncle surveyed a pasture to the right that rose away from the road. He finally stopped when he located scattered clusters of cedar trees of varying sizes near the top. We didn't have any Christmas tree farms in the region nor did we import trees from the outside. We made do with what we had, that is red cedars, and there were plenty for everyone. Probably no one in our area paid for a Christmas tree. Everyone knew friends or relatives with plots or fields from which they could cut a cedar. In fact, my father always cut our tree from a rocky back corner of the eleven acre small farm upon which we lived, located a hundred yards south of the city limits of Thayer, Missouri, on highway 63. The region was covered with forests, but the trees were all deciduous except for the ubiquitous cedars.

It was not difficult to locate cedars about seven feet tall and shaped much like the traditional Christmas trees in the scattered groves that afternoon. Soon we found four to our liking, one for the Martins, one for my Taylor grandparents, one for the Dunsmores and finally one for Uncle Cleo and Aunt Ova. Uncle Cleo and Bynum cut the trees with a hand saw. We carried them to the pickup with an adult at the trunk and one of us boys following with a firm grip on the crest. After loading the trees in the back James Ray and I climbed in. My uncle turned around at the entrance to the farm, and we headed back to the Martin's. On the way we sang Christmas songs in an effort to drown out the noise of the pickup.

By time we were teenagers James Ray was called Jim and I Tom. But it was typical for younger southern Missouri boys to be addressed by both names, especially when parents hoped to curtail rowdiness. My parents never called me Tom. To them I was Thomas. My father asserted that "tom is a male cat," nor did he like Tommy.

Ozark Christmas in 1936

CHRISTMAS IN THE OZARKS

The Christmas season in our region of the Ozarks, Oregon County, Missouri, and Fulton County, Arkansas, and the towns of Thayer, Missouri, and Mammoth Spring, Arkansas, just across the state line from each other, reflected the larger 1930 societal trends in America. Information about the larger culture was readily available for those who attended movies, listened to the radio, and read newspapers and magazines. Perhaps the *Saturday Evening Post, Reader's Digest* and educational journals for teachers were the major disseminators of new trends to those in our area. Certain distinctives, however, prevailed. Persons of Scotch-Irish American Protestant stock made up the majority of the inhabitants in our part of the Ozarks. Their forefathers had immigrated westward from the Carolinas, Kentucky, Tennessee, and Alabama. Some pursued a more northerly route through Ohio, Indiana, and Illinois. Few persons of other nationalities or Roman Catholics lived in the region and no racial minorities. There were, however, scattered German and Swiss families. Holiday times were family occasions, mostly of the immediate family. Regardless, extended families must also be considered since larger networks sometimes came into play. At the turn of the last century large families of around ten children were the norm. The result was that numerous persons married into other extended families and were interlaced into the larger overlaying networks.

My family consisted of Scotch-Irish, English and German components. But culturally and religiously we were most influenced by the first two since these were the relatives with whom we spent the most time. For that reason I will first focus upon our British ancestors, then turn to the German influences.

GATHERING NUTS

Actually the harbinger of Christmas in our nuclear family was even earlier than the cutting of Christmas trees. The gathering of nuts in October and November was the real precursor. My family consisted of my father, Ben Olbricht, my mother, Agnes Taylor Olbricht, and my siblings Nedra, Glenn and Owen. I was the second child. All were involved in gathering nuts and picking out meats except for my father. Southeast of the barn out in the cow pasture we had three hickories in a row on the high side of an incline and lower toward a small stream four native black walnut trees. These nuts were very important to my mother, for from them we created Christmas gifts for her immediate family. 1936 was the heart of the Depression and money was not easy to come upon. My mother gave her parents and siblings nut-meats, along with nut-filled fudge and divinity. Mother made divinity by whipping egg whites into granulated sugar and corn syrup and adding vanilla and nuts. We had plenty of eggs because we kept hens.

My father had money, in part, because he did not spend anymore than absolutely necessary. He did not marry until he was forty-one. He homesteaded in Sioux County, Nebraska, in 1906 at age 21. By time he married he owned 1440 acres of Nebraska ranchland. The demand for potatoes rose during World War I, and for the time and place he prospered through his potatoes. In 1936 everything he owned was fully paid for. He had money in the bank and in government savings bonds. Around Thayer he worked at many odd jobs including building houses, painting, finishing floors, erecting windmills, and helping out at my grandfather's gas station.

My father's parents bought a farm east of Thayer in 1910 and moved from Nebraska. When dad came by train to visit his parents he transported potatoes in a boxcar to sell along the way. He got to know my grandfather Taylor through selling potatoes to him. My grandfather often purchased large lots of various items including apples, watermelons, and potatoes and sold them at his small grocery.

My grandfather introduced my forty-year-old bachelor father to his twenty-nine year "old-maid schoolteacher" daughter. After a year or so of corresponding and visiting, my mother and father married in April 1927. We had adequate resources on which to live from my father's work and from the fact that we grew about everything we ate—vegetables, grain, fruit, dairy products and chickens. My father had additional income through leasing out the Nebraska ranch. Despite our circumstances my mother felt compelled to prepare these gifts for her relatives because my father did not wish to expend any money.

When the nuts began to fall in late October my mother instructed my sister Nedra, and younger brothers Glenn and Owen, and me in how to pick up the nuts and haul them back to the house about a hundred fifty yards away. To a seven year old, however, that seemed almost a mile. We had a Red Ryder wagon that was probably a gift from a previous Christmas. We also took along two-gallon buckets into which we threw the nuts. When the buckets were full we set them on the wagon and headed back to the house. It was uphill most of the way, but the incline was gradual and modest. Either my sister or I pulled, and my brothers pushed. We used the Red Ryder for about everything both in playing and working. The heat in our house came from a wood stove in the large dining room. My daily job was to haul wood from a large pile located near the barn about a hundred feet from the back of the house. I then had to carry it up five steps and stack it on the back porch.

We never had many children's vehicles. I seem to recall having a tricycle that we handed down to our siblings. Our father never bought us a bike. It may have had something to do with the expenditure, but his explanation was that it was dangerous to ride a bike along the highway. He kept telling us that we could get killed. That indeed was a real possibility since highway 63 on which we lived had steady traffic, was not very wide, and possessed gravel shoulders.

Normally we started with the hickory nuts. Their hulls split off in sections and were fairly easy to remove. One of the hickory trees was different. The nuts were larger and shaped like a somewhat deflated football. They were considerably easier to remove from the shells, and we kids preferred to work on them. The two other trees produced round nuts with smaller meats. They were difficult to remove even with a nut pick. We had to be very careful about removing small particles of shell because it was quite painful to chomp down on these hard bits. Uncle Norval complained to my mother that he was not too fond of her gifts because of the pieces of shell in both the meats and the candy.

We brought the walnuts to the house somewhat later preferably after the first frost. One tree had larger meats and was especially easy to process. Once it frosted most of the nuts fell. We seldom tried to knock them off the trees. We loaded the walnuts on the wagon with their hulls on. We took them up to the driveway and scattered them across the ruts. When my father left in the morning or came home at night he ran over the nuts and the weight forced the hulls off the shells.

Our land was all fenced in. The garage was east of the well house that was located ten feet back of the house. The well house had a concrete vat in which to place milk, cream and butter in the summer so as to keep them cool. It also had a large storage area. A windmill tower went through the roof, and the blade thirty feet up pumped the water. My father built a concrete covered water tank on the high point of our property in front of the house toward the highway. The windmill pumped the water to the tank, and our house supply came back down by gravity. The garage was located on the other side or east of the well house. My father always put our 1932 Chevrolet four door sedan in the garage. To get to the garage one drove about 100 feet past the house south and turned into the culverted entry. We had to open a wood-framed , wire-covered gate in order to enter our property. It was designed to keep the cows off the highway. We kids were expected to watch for our father's arrival after work and open the gate. He usually was able to tell us the approximate time and that depended upon what he was doing and the distance he had to drive. The first segment of the grassed-over driveway went just north of our red barn for about a hundred feet where we kept milk cows, chickens, hay, and feed. The area just north of the driveway was fenced to keep the cows out of the orchards and vegetable gardens. A second gate on this fence of the same type was located east of the barn. The driveway at that point took a ninety-degree angle to the north, and it was about fifty feet to the garage. When my father arrived we met him at the first gate. One of us closed it while a second raced ahead to open the second gate. It was on the segment north of the second gate toward the garage upon which we spread the walnuts.

Once the car tires crushed the hulls we picked up the walnuts. That was a very difficult job if one wished to avoid stained hands. At first I was not very careful, and I discovered that it took at least three weeks for the stain to wear away. I was especially embarrassed at school so I kept my hands in my pockets as much as possible. Everyone, even the teacher commented, "You've been hulling walnuts, haven't you?" It would have helped to have rubber gloves, but my father was not about to buy rubber gloves. After we picked up the walnuts we laid them out to dry in our dirt-floored cellar. Sometime in late November we commenced cracking the nuts and picking out the meats. Normally my father, but sometimes my mother, cracked several nuts on our cement steps with a hammer and put them in a bucket or a round aluminum pan about a foot across and three inches deep. We then used nut picks to work out the meats. It was a tedious job and required far more patience than possessed by a seven-year old. My mother was pretty good at various strategies to keep us working. Sometimes she read to us while we worked. At other times she set goals of so many cups of meats or minutes after which we could quit and go play. I'm not so sure our relatives appreciated our hard-attained gifts, but at least we were well aware that they cost us considerable monotonous effort. About the middle of December my mother started making fudge and divinity. We kids picked up the broken squares of fudge and misshapen pieces of divinity as a reward. My mother packaged the best for our grandparents, her siblings and spouses and single siblings.

CHRISTMAS AT OUR HOUSE

My father always waited until at least the week before Christmas before he cut our tree. Sometimes he invited us to go with him to the back of the cow pasture to cut it. Once we had it home he nailed together a cross-piece of one by fours and drove a sixteen penny nail through the base and into the tree. He then set the tree by the wall away from the windows. My father considered his job done when he placed the tree in the living room. My mother supervised the decoration. We had to exercise creativity in constructing decorations because my father objected to expenses for ornaments. At my grandfather Taylor's, however, it was different. He always bought tree decorations sometimes wholesale from the distributors. My grandmother and aunts took decorations out the storage boxes and put them on the tree including several glass blown ornaments, red and green lights, and narrow cut aluminum tinsel. They also had continuous red fluffy ropes to wrap about the tree from the bottom to the top.

We had none of these commercial ornaments. We made popcorn balls out of syrup, or molasses, let them dry, ran a string through the middle, and circled these on the outer edge of the branches. My mother put us kids to work making linked paper circles that we colored red, orange and green before gluing the circles together into a chain. These we also circled around the tree from top to bottom. We made a large star and covered it with tinfoil and put it on the crown. Our tree wasn't impressive, but at least it was our tree because we invested considerable effort on decorations. Preparing for Christmas was a busy and special time. What we did from the middle of December until after the beginning of January certainly broke from the routines of the rest of the year.

Despite the fact that our father eschewed talk about what we might get for Christmas that didn't prevent my siblings and me from discussing our gift lists. Sometime in the fall we received mail order catalogues from Montgomery Ward and Sears and Roebuck. Our parents left these catalogues on a shelf and therefore they were accessible to us kids. Why they left them available probably is that we occupied many hours pouring through the catalogues when inclement weather prevented us from going outside. We normally received new clothes in the fall just before school began. In the case of my brothers and me we normally received two new pairs of overalls, a couple of new shirts, one being long sleeved, a new pair of shoes and new socks. These were to last us for the school year, but if it seemed that we needed more clothes we would likely get, for example, a new shirt at Christmas time. Our clothing was almost always ordered from the Montgomery Ward catalogue because it was presumed that the catalogue items cost less than purchasing them from the Olds Dry Goods Store in downtown Thayer.

I don't know that Montgomery Ward sold merchandise for less than Sears and Roebuck, but their orders were shipped from Kansas City, while the latter shipped out of Chicago. Another reason we ordered from Montgomery Ward was that our grandfather Olbricht owned stock in the company. Before Christmas we checked out the clothing and toy sections of the catalogue, especially the latter, pouring over the games such as spinning tops, Tinker Toys, and Lincoln logs while our sister carefully considered all sorts of dolls. We dreamed and schemed for the latest in each case. We would mention these aloud as much for the benefit of our father as for each other and he often overheard us. He had an interesting way of defusing our wishes. He spoke out in a loud voice, "Well, if you want it cut it out!" as if the picture was equivalent to actual possession. I think though that we may have received an occasional toy from our parents. I remember that we seemed to get a new set of Tinker Toys, a more advanced set every Christmas. I think our parents ordered certain of these items. My mother probably saw to it that we received intellectually challenging toys that occupied several hours during the day.

We had checkers but that demanded only two players. Four of us could not be occupied at the same time so that we had difficulty arranging for ourselves who would play when. Another game we probably had as early as 1936 was Chinese Checkers. Six could play, and my mother loved to play with us at night when she was free from household duties. My father never joined in any games. Chinese checkers or Chinker Checks as we sometimes called them were a bit advanced for my youngest brother Owen who turned four when I was seven, but we helped him.

The game that really occupied our time was Monopoly. I don't recall when we first received a set, probably from one of our mother's siblings at Christmas time. Monopoly was the rage in 1936. Parker Brothers purchased Monopoly in 1934 and they commenced major marketing of the game in 1935. By Christmas of 1936 versions of the game were sold throughout the world and especially as Christmas gifts in America. If we did receive the game that Christmas it occupied much of our time even more than our father preferred. We could not play it quietly and my father, who normally went to bed by 9:30, insisted that we stop before he tried to sleep. The game was a bit complicated, but with our help even Owen was able to play. We often played outdoor games such as marbles, softball, and football with neighborhood kids our age in our pasture or in the Phelps' to the south, but almost never indoor games with our male neighbors. Since our sister was the only girl she was permitted to invite friends over to play dolls in her bedroom, but we guys almost never had boys come in the house.

CHRISTMAS AT SCHOOL AND CHURCH

As Christmas approached we had a few special activities at Thayer Elementary School. These are not nearly as vivid to me, however, some seventy years later. I recall being involved in a skit before Thanksgiving. Dorris Hackett was my second grade teacher. The skit involved Miles Standish wooing Priscilla Mullins, based upon Henry Wadsworth Longfellow's *The Courtship of Miles Standish*. I played John Alden and delivered Standish's request of marriage to Priscilla's father. When the father sought out Priscilla and asked her disposition she replied in the famous line, "Why don't you speak for yourself, John?" I only appeared in the skit one time and had these few lines. We also had a skit at Christmas time based upon Charles Dickens, *A Christmas Carol*. Since I was the largest boy in class I played Bob Cratchit and carried Tiny Tim played by the smallest boy in class. My memory is that I had few lines. We had a decorated Christmas tree in our assembly hall and stringed green or red fuzzy ropes across the room three feet below the ceiling. If we did a Christmas skit that year I was not involved.

An indelible memory, however, is that we exchanged gifts in our classroom by drawing names. We were to purchase a present for the person whose name we drew but not tell them. The gift giver was to be the surprise when the presents were exchanged. The gift was not to cost more than $.25 but most were in the $.10 category. Much could be purchased in 1936 for $.25. One could buy a small Baby Ruth, Snickers, or Butterfinger candy bar for $.01. On the last day before the Christmas holiday we brought our gifts and placed them in a large container near a small Christmas tree. Two or three persons picked out to be Santa's helpers distributed the gifts toward the close of the day. They read the names then took the present to the recipient. The name of the person purchasing the gift was enclosed. The teacher always had two or three gifts available just in case one was missing because of a failure to bring one or because a student was absent. Gifts ranged from candy and Cracker Jacks to toy cars, cutout dolls, and tops. Most of items were purchased at the Benjamin Franklin 5 and 10 in downtown Thayer. The parents of one of my classmates, Sammy Simmons, managed the 5 and 10. Sammy later graduated from college and spent time in the army. Afterward he received a law degree from Harvard Law School and became a vice president and legal counsel for the Revelon Corporation. My impression was that my classmates were about as interested in who bought their gift as they were in the gift itself. From the nature of the present students speculated as to how well they were liked by the purchaser.

The celebration of Christmas where we went to church was another matter. My parents and many relatives on both sides were members of the Churches of Christ. The Churches of Christ in the Ozarks persisted in the traditional American religious traditions regarding holidays going back to the Puritans. The Puritans rejected religious celebrations as misdirected innovations that sprang up in the medieval churches indebted to the Pagan holidays. The Puritans did not celebrate Easter or Christmas. The same was true three centuries later of many American Protestant denominations especially in the rural areas. We did nothing in our local Churches of Christ to celebrate Christmas, not even to sing carols. In fact, it was fairly typical on the Sunday before Christmas to preach on why Christmas should not be celebrated. The reasons given were that there is nothing to encourage such celebrations in the Scriptures, that the precise dates of Christ's birth and resurrection are unknown, and that these holidays have Pagan origins. The claim was that there is no reason to believe that Christ was born on December 25 since sheep were in the pastures, making a spring date more likely. That specific day was selected by third century Christians, in part because it coincided with the pagan festivals celebrating Saturnalia and the winter solstice. Some of the members of the Church of Christ where we attended in Mammoth Spring did not celebrate Christmas in home settings at all but several did. Those who did so declared Christmas a family holiday and not a religious or church one. Our extended family never questioned the family celebration of Christmas. We did not even mention its religious significance though we sometimes sang the religious Christmas carols. We took Christ out of Christmas for Christian reasons, not as now commonly claimed for secular ones.

Ozark Christmas in 1936

CHRISTMAS AT MY MATERNAL GRANDPARENTS

In 1936 my mother's siblings consisted of two unmarried sisters, both of whom taught vocational home economics, Bertha Taylor in Smithville, Missouri, north of Kansas City and Alice Taylor who taught at Thayer High. Mother had three brothers. The oldest was Norval. My mother and all her siblings graduated from Southwest Missouri State Teachers College, now Missouri State at Springfield, except Norval. Uncle Norval attended, as I recall for three years, but at that point he was offered a job he decided he could not refuse. Standard Oil of Indiana (now Exxon) offered him the agency for all of Oregon County. The position involved delivering gas and oil products to all the Standard Oil stations in the county. My grandfather owned a Standard Oil station located on Highway 63 between Thayer and Mammoth beginning in 1922. Mother's brother Cleo lived in Alton, Missouri, where he taught vocational agriculture at Alton High. He also commenced farming on the side, first by renting, then buying land. Mother's youngest brother, twenty-one years younger than my mother, was Wellington Taylor, who in the middle 1950s began going by the name Tom. His full name was Wellington Thomas Taylor. In 1936 he was a student at Southwest Missouri. Aunt Bertha and Uncle Wellington came home at Christmas time, and all of us gathered for Christmas activities at the home of T. Shelt and Myrtle Taylor, my grandparents.

The arrival of my Uncle Wellington before Christmas heralded another Christmas time activity. My grandfather T. Shelt loved to play the card game Pitch. It was the most exciting with four players. In 1936 my grandfather's great nephew, Albert Prewitt, stayed with him to finish high school. He helped out on the farm feeding beef cattle and taking care of the gas station/grocery, now called a convenience store. Albert's parents lived east of Wirth, Arkansas about ten miles. It was very difficult to attend high school if he stayed at home. He was our fourth hand for Pitch in a bidding game that identifies a trump, the bidder discarding the number of extra cards taken from the kitty, and each trick counting a point.

My grandfather was normally the winner. He almost always bid regardless, and he was lucky. Since I was perceived to be the weakest player I paired with my grandfather. Uncle Wellington and Albert were partners. After a period of coaching I got to where I was pretty good. My grandfather had to have unusual patience because though he loved to win he did not get upset with me while I was learning. More than once because of early blunders I caused us to unnecessarily lose a few games. It was possible to shoot the moon if one perceived that he could take all the tricks. When you shoot the moon you either win it all or lose it all. One time I was almost certain I could take all the tricks, and I declared that I would shoot the moon. Unfortunately, my grandfather didn't have any helping cards, and I lost two tricks, which meant we lost my bid, and that was deducted from our score. We sometimes played until 2:00 A. M. in the morning. I stayed with my grandfather during that period. My parents would never let me stay up that long.

In 1936 the Taylor family got together on Christmas Eve to exchange gifts then came back together to eat a large meal on Christmas day. My sense was that this was rather common in our region. I'm not exactly sure of the backgrounds of the Taylor family Christmas. I think it evolved over the years influenced by radio and newspaper accounts and commercialism. I suspect that several area family Christmases were much the same though there were individual family preferences.

My grandmother Taylor was born in Ionia, Michigan, in 1879. Her father Albert Dunsmore served in a Michigan regiment in the Civil War. He volunteered when he was underage and was designated the company bugler. When his age was discovered he was given an honorable discharge. He later reenlisted. He moved his family to Missouri about 1885 and lived 10 miles east of Thayer near Rose Hill. I am not aware of what specific traditions Myrtle Dunsmore Taylor may have brought to Christmas. Her cooking was basically southern probably in order to please the tastes of my grandfather who had very definite views of what he wanted to eat. He loved southern staples such as fried chicken and pork chops, white gravy, bacon, sausage and eggs, black-eyed peas, mustard greens, and turnips. But he also ate a large variety of items out of cans especially when grandma was gone, including salmon, sardines, hot tamales and chili, and Vienna sausages. Most northerners made turkey dressing out of white wheat bread. grandma made dressing out of corn bread as did almost everyone else in southern Missouri.

Christmas Eve 1936 after we ate our supper at home we gathered with our Taylor Grandparents and mother's siblings for the exchanging of gifts. At that time most everyone had gifts for everyone else though only a single gift might go to a married couple. We heard that Santa was coming to the house that night. After a time of waiting we heard a loud knock on the front door and a "ho, ho, ho"! Uncle Wellington went to the door, opened it and in walked a large Santa. Because of his hat he looked exceptionally tall. It was a numinous moment. My two brothers were frightened, and I didn't feel comfortable. He went over to the lighted Christmas tree and started picking up gifts and distributing them. My brothers and I were somewhat reluctant to reach and out take the gifts from him. After awhile it dawned on me that the Santa must be Uncle Norval, and I felt less threatened. I surmised this first because he wasn't with Aunt Mabel but then I decided Santa talked like him. He made a good Santa. He was five nine and weighed two hundred thirty pounds. He filled out the suit without pillows. He was in good shape despite being on the heavy side. He regularly lifted 55 gallon barrels of motor oil that weighed above 400 pounds. When he had finishing distributing the gifts he waved to everyone and with a "ho, ho, ho" departed out the front door. About fifteen minutes later Uncle Norval walked in. He explained that he was late because he had to make an emergency gas delivery. A few years later I discovered the Santa suit in an attic closet at my grandparents' house.

It's too long ago for me to recall who received what gifts that Christmas. I do recall vividly, however, distribution of the packages of nuts and candy we prepared. I also recall that we each received a cord-woven bag of nuts and oranges from grandfather's store. The nuts were pecans, English walnuts, almonds, hazel and Brazil nuts, designated in that era "nigger toes," all unshelled. Sometimes he included a coconut for each family.

Since my siblings and I were the only grandkids we received gifts from all the adults, some individual and some for all of us to play with. I recall a large metal top that when the screw -like grooved shaft was pushed down all the way the top spun rapidly. If one pushed it down vigorously three or four times then released the top, it would spin independently for four or five minutes. I recall metal jack-in-the -boxes that were about five inches square. It was fun to sneak up on someone and release the catch. I remember sets of jacks and bags of marbles. I recall various board games and perhaps the gift of a softball and bat. Nedra our sister often received dolls and cardboard doll cutouts. We also received clothing, but that was likely from our parents.

The extended Taylor family was accustomed to eating together most Sunday noons following church services. We ate dinner at the fairly large house of T. Shelt and Myrtle Taylor. My mother's two brothers Norval and Cleo and spouses were normally present, as well as her unmarried home economics teacher sister, Alice. Sometimes Bynum and Opal Dunsmore, along with James Ray joined us. Bynum's parents both died while he was a teenager. His father was grandma Taylor's brother, and his mother was the sister of T. Shelt Taylor. Bynam's oldest sister Pearl kept the family together, but my grandparents had some hand in raising him. The adults always ate first. Weather permitting we played outside until we were called, for example, hide and seek or follow the leader. When we were older we played football. The adults didn't hurry any because they engaged in extended conversations. If Bynum was present he always had news about happenings he picked up at the barbershop. By time we were called for dinner we were always hungry since it might be 1:30 P. M. We never worried about the food running out because there was always more than we could eat even if some of the items might be mostly gone.

The women all brought food, normally the same item week after week. The meat was often fried chicken, but sometimes ham, meat loaf, pork chops, or roast beef. We sometimes had more than one kind. Especially in the summer we had lots of vegetables since about everyone had a garden except our grandparents. We had leaf lettuce, tomatoes, peas, cowpeas, baked beans, green beans, kohl rabi, spinach, carrots, radishes, green onions, sweet corn, squash, turnips, and potatoes. In winter we ate many of these vegetables from canned Mason glass jars. Various women baked their favorite cakes and pies. The specialty of Aunt Ova was sweet potato chunks baked with pineapple and topped with marshmallows. That was my favorite. The same menu was likely for Christmas dinner in the canned versions, but the meat was turkey.

Ordinarily my grandfather bought the turkey, but for a couple of years we raised some in his woods. We soon discovered that the hens did not sit on the eggs so as to hatch them efficiently So we removed the eggs from their nets and took them to the hatchery. It was my job to watch the hens from a distance and see where they disappeared. They hid their nests in clumps of grass and around brush piles. The hens were dedicated to eluding animals that might wish to devour their eggs. I learned how to watch them patiently and then go discover the hens upon their nests. Later when they left I would collect the eggs.

CHRISTMAS AT MY FRATERNAL GRANDPARENTS

The Christmas celebration was considerably different in the Henry and Bertha Olbricht family. They lived on a five-hundred-acre farm twelve miles east of Thayer, up and over Eldorado hill. By time I knew them my grandfather was in his late seventies and the farm had been taken over by their son Ted along with his family. We only went to see them three or four times a year, and I recall the grandparents coming to see us only once. I recall one Christmas when my grandfather attended mass at the small white wooden framed Catholic Church on the street south of the main street in Thayer. Afterward he, my grandmother, Uncle Ted, and Aunt Vernie dropped by to see us for an hour or two. My grandfather did not attend mass regularly. As I recall a priest came from West Plains to do the service. grandma Olbricht was a Lutheran.

My grandfather Olbricht was born in 1856 in what was then Glatz in the German province of Silesia. That city, designated Klodzko, since post World War II is now located in southwestern Poland. Grandfather completed parochial school and then apprenticed as a tanner. He was from a large family. Two of his older brothers immigrated to New York City in the early 1870s. When he was twenty had he stayed in Germany he would have been drafted into the Prussian army for two years of service. Instead he traveled Europe picking up tanning jobs in different cities. Rather than returning to Glatz and being drafted into the military at age twenty-two, he immigrated to the United States shipping out of Bremerhaven.

In the United States he settled in Elizabeth, New Jersey, because several tanning companies were located along the Hudson. He married German immigrant Kathrine Eich from Regensburg. They had four children, including the third, my father. Katherine Eick Olbricht died when my father was four in 1889. One of my grandfather's brothers, at the instigation of a cousin, had by then moved to Sioux County, Nebraska, and homesteaded. My grandfather being somewhat at loose ends decided to join him as a homesteader in this northwest Nebraska County, filing in 1892. His wife's sister took over the care of the four children for a year. Unfortunately his Nebraska brother Joseph was killed a few years later while moving a house. The wife of Joseph, Matilda Lange Olbricht, had a sister Bertha who lived in Denver and served as a cook for the family of a mining tycoon. Matilda introduced Bertha to my grandfather. Bertha was previously married to a German named Sauser. He died shortly thereafter leaving her with a son named Ernest. She was born in a German -speaking settlement in Eastern Europe that was sometimes in Russia and sometimes in Poland. After the marriage of Henry and Bertha, Ernest lived with them. A few years earlier, grandfather's brother and wife brought children by the previous marriage by train to western Nebraska. In 1901 a son, Theodore or Ted, was born.

Missouri Memories, 1934–1947

I don't recall that we ever visited the Olbrichts at Christmas and that family's gift exhange. I do recall, however, once during a Christmas season that Ted's, Ernest's and our family gathered for a night meal at Uncle Ted and Aunt Vernie's. Their house was about 200 feet from that of the Olbricht grandparents, and the grandparents were there as well. All of the Olbrichts and Sausers living in Missouri were therefore present. Ernest Sauser's wife was the older sister of Bynum Dunsmore and therefore the double cousin of my mother. Even the Olbrichts were an intertwined family. The wife of Uncle Ted, Vernie Pauli Olbricht, had a brother Adolph Pauli who was married to one of mother's Dunsmore cousins, Lucy Dunsmore Pauli.

In 1936 my father and mother packed us four kids into the 1932 Chevrolet Sudan for a Christmas season trip to the Olbricht farm. Though it was only 12 miles it took over an hour. The roads were all dirt and not too well maintained. Ruts developed as the result of the freezing and thawing common at that time of the year. Because of sharp rocks it was not uncommon to have a flat. When that happened we all ascended from the car and either helped dad or roamed around in the woods. He always carried a cold patch kit to repair the inner tubes. One time, fortunately in the summer, we had two flats returning home.

We entered the farm about a quarter mile from the house. We had to open a wood-framed wire gate like those on the way to our garage. We always drove past Uncle Ted's house on up to our grandparents. Grandmother, the professional cook, was famous for her cookies and cakes. She normally offered us some soon after we arrived. If the weather was suitable we were told to play outside. That was fine with us. Uncle Ted and Aunt Vernie had adopted a brother and sister somewhat older than us, and we played with them. There were paths to explore and ponds to visit. We could always go to the barn through the grape arbor to see the horses or cattle.

My grandparents spoke German to each other even when we were there. But they spoke English with my father and Uncle Ted. Ted spoke a bit of German. The three men sat around and talked about Nebraska days. My father took a weekly newspaper from Harrison and Crawford, Nebraska, and kept up with people and events there. My mother visited with the women. My grandfather rarely talked to us children. Perhaps he felt uncomfortable since we had some difficulty understanding his Germanic accent. About the only way in which he took notice of us was in playing some of his records for us. He had a hand-winding Victor Victrola floor model record player and a collection of several 78 records in brown paper covers. His favorite records or at least those he played for us were his Uncle Josh records. These were recordings made by Calvin Edward Stewart (1856–1919) featuring a farmer who gets involved city life and manners. I liked especially the record, "Uncle Josh at the Dentist's" recorded in 1909. He also had a recording of the German folk song "Die Lorelei" that he always played for us and as I recall sometimes with tears in his eyes. He only returned to Germany once along with grandmother in order to visit his sister and brother and families. That was fifty years after he came to the United States, 1928, a year before I was born.

My step-grandmother baked several varieties of cookies, some American, but a few of them German. I preferred cookies or pastries containing marzipan. But my favorite at Christmas time was Pfeffernuse. (A literal English translation is pepper nuts) I usually ate more of those than pleased my father. Bertha Olbricht died in 1955. Both my wife and I liked her Pfeffernuse so much that we obtained the recipe from my Aunt Vernie, and Dorothy regularly makes these delectable German specialties at Christmas time. Grandma made a flat cake or coffee cake which she called streuenkucken. The German word may be translated sprinkle cake. It was a regular white cake with cinnamon and brown sugar mixed with butter and sprinkled on top. She cooked with lots of butter because they milked several cows and made their own butter. She also made German fruit torts. I don't recall anything else distinctively German in her meals but occasionally she served Sauerbraten (roasted marinated beef). Aunt Vernie's rolls were the best I ever ate.

I don't recall that my German grandparents ever gave us presents, but my grandmother packed up enough cookies for a week to take home if our mother and father could keep us out of them. My grandfather made his own sausages and packed them link fashion in the standard sheep guts. I was not too impressed with his regular wurst that was something like coarse ground bratwurst. But I loved his liver sausage or leberwurst. It has never been possible to find liver sausage in America that tastes like his, though the Oscar Meyer liver sausage loaf encased in a layer of fat comes close. But I have bought such small encasement liver sausages in groceries in St. Petersburg, Russia, that taste just like his. Mother also took nuts, fudge and divinity to the Olbricht relatives.

The height of the visit at my German grandparents was the opening of a box from my grandfather's brother Benjamin and his family who lived in New York City. They never came to visit us in Missouri. He died in 1938.

He operated a jewelry shop in Manhattan. My father while younger and single visited them a few times in New York. I know there were gifts in the box that I'm sure included jewelry for the women. Perhaps there were tie tacks and chains, along with cuff links for the men. I know there were a few toys, but I don't recall what they were specifically. What I anticipated most and what fixed indelibly in my memory was that they saved up the Sunday comics for the year and sent them in the package. I loved comics. We had funnies in the *Springfield Daily News* to which my grandfather subscribed. But the New York paper, perhaps the *New York Herald*, contained several additional ones. I loved especially the Katzenjammer Kids, Jiggs and Maggie, Little Abner, Dick Tracey, Buck Rogers, and Felix the Cat. We were permitted to take these comics home. I read them over and over until they grew so ragged my father made me throw them out.

The Christmas experience at the Olbrichts was not long, nevertheless memorable. The lasting factor was the fictional world of the comics which was sometimes as real to me as our Ozarks environment. I was proud of my German heritage and spoke of it in school whenever Germany came up. That was to change, however, in 1941 when the United States declared war on Germany.

AFTER CHRISTMAS

After Christmas was over Uncle Wellington Taylor set up his electric train in the least-used of the double living rooms in my grandparent's house. It was the regular HO scale. He had about twenty feet of track and stations, houses,and other buildings to position along the way. If there was a Christmas gift to which I aspired but never received it was an electric train. I could, however, play with my Uncle's train when it was up, but that was not often because he was away at college and mostly set it up at Christmas time. I was not permitted to set it up on my own even when I lived with my grandparents after the third grade. They only lived a half mile from my parents,and I went home rather regularly. I helped my Grandfather pump gas and sell groceries and cigarettes. We actually pumped gas manually into a ten gallon round tall glass tank at the top of the pump. The gas descended by gravity into the car tank. I recall that when we got electric pumps we could not sell gas when the power was off. We never had that problem with the manual pumps.

Ozark Christmas in 1936

My uncle also had other items I never owned, for example a baseball glove, a tennis racket, a football, golf clubs, and roller skates with steel wheels that attached to regular shoes. All of these I was permitted to play with though I never went to a tennis court to use the racket. My grandfather permitted men of Thayer and Mammoth who loved golf to build a nine-hole course on his forty-acre farm. Because of irregular maintenance the course had sand-greens. Used motor oil was mixed with the sand to keep the dust down and to compress the surface. The greens had rollers and levelers. One was permitted to create a path to the cup from where the ball landed on the green. It was also often necessary to clean the "cow pies" off the green since grandpa ran a herd of beef cattle on the land. Soon after age seven I caddied, as he called it, for the rural delivery mailman Slats Smith from Mammoth Spring. Occasionally I used my uncle's clubs to play few holes on my own, sometimes accompanied by my brothers. I was also permitted to use the roller skates. About the only place we had to roller skate was the sidewalk leading from the house to the gas station! It was slightly down hill and about thirty feet in length. I with my brothers learned to skate down to the store, but never really mastered skating back up.

Uncle Wellington prepared to teach vocational agriculture at Southwest Missouri and the University of Missouri. He was much more interested in wood working than in farming and was always making useful items. He made a wooden rack for distributing cigarette packages that we filled at the top and removed at the bottom. That made it much more convenient and worked quite well. One Christmas he made me a wooden replica of a stub-nosed truck and trailer on the order of today's eighteen wheelers. He used six skate wheels, four on the truck and two on the trailer. The trailer was sturdy enough for us to place our feet in and reach down and guide the tractor down the sidewalk. Both my brothers and I spent much time going up and down the sidewalk. We always looked forward to the return of Uncle Wellington from college. He often played with us. One summer he taught us gymnastics, a course he took in college. That all went well until he lay on his back and with his feet launched me into the air in order to complete a summersault before I landed. Unfortunately one time he flipped me into a tree truck and broke the small bone in my left arm. Our parents strongly recommended that we discontinue the gymnastic lessons.

Uncle Wellington also possessed a sled. As I recall later in the thirties, either my father or one of our Uncles bought us a sled so that now we had two. We never had much snow in our area. Normally it would last at most for two or three days. We had a slope in the southwest corner of our field at home and one on Uncle Cleo's land that was contiguous with grandfather Taylor's. If we packed a path we could slide for a considerable distance, perhaps two hundred feet, on Uncle Cleo's land. My brothers and I hit the slope as often as possible. In the winter of 1941 we had a snow that lasted for three weeks. That winter the large Standard oil thermometer at my grandfather's gas station registered twenty-four below zero one night. That was very unusual.

The Christmas season came to a close when the schools started back up after New Years. We didn't celebrate New Years in any special way in our family. We didn't even stay up to see the New Year in. The towns blew their fire sirens at midnight, and some people lighted firecrackers or shot rifles in the air, but we usually slept through and didn't hear all the commotion. My grandfather closed down his store on Christmas day unless someone knocked on his door to purchase gas or groceries. But he stayed open New Years.

Christmas time was a welcome reprieve from the routines of the rest of the year. The middle 1930s in the Ozarks were halcyon years. We pretty much ignored the wars looming in Europe and hoped for non-involvement. World War I was still fresh in the minds of those who lived through it and who served in the military. For a few days after classes started up I went through something like withdrawal symptoms. But they did not last. School now took up time, including school lot football at recess that I enjoyed very much. At night we played the new board games and looked forward to the breezes of March when we could fly kites. We didn't get everything we wished for at Christmas, but we never felt unwanted or neglected. We were warmly accepted by all in our extended family. We always kept busy and mother saw to it that we had plenty of books to read by taking us to the public library regularly where we could check out three books each.

The next fall after the long months of summer vacation we anticipated another Christmas. Life moved through repeated cycles until 1941 when war broke out and adolescence arrived bringing with it budding gender relationships rivaling Christmas in intensity.

Chapter IV

Later Depression Years

ROOSEVELT "NEW DEAL" PROGRAMS

Several Depression years programs impacted the workmen of our region. Three important labor intensive programs were the CCC (Civilian Conservation Corps), the WPA (Works Progress Administration) and PWA (Public Works Administration).

The CCC was launched as a part of Franklin Roosevelt's New Deal in 1933 and continued until 1944, in the middle of World War II. Normally, those signing up for the Corps were from families below a certain income level. These men lived in camps (and sometimes tents) in national and state parks. The camp in Oregon County was at Bardley, east of Alton, and almost to the Ripley County line. Their assigned tasks were to improve these designated lands by planting trees, building roads and trails, camping facilities and sports areas. Their impact on improvement of the environment was considerable. They were furnished with food, clothing, and shelter in addition to pay of $30 a month. It was required, however, that they send $25 a month home to help support their disadvantaged family. None of my extended family was in CCC, though we saw groups of these men traveling in working uniforms in open transportation trucks on the county roads. They sometimes stopped at my grandfather's gas station to purchase candy and cigarettes. Most of the northeastern area of Oregon County was located within the Mark Twain National Forest, and the CCC had continuous assignments there.

Oregon County always voted Democratic in those years. No county officials were Republicans. Though Republicans might be on the ballot they never received more than about a fourth of the total vote. However, a number of the Democrats in the county opposed features of the New Deal. They argued that Roosevelt was spending too much of the taxpayers' hard earned money. The general feeling was that though incomes were low in our region they would be boosted little by the various NDeal programs. None of my relatives apparently qualified for these programs since they were farmers, small businessmen, carpenters, stone masons, or educators and kept fully occupied. In terms of camp life and discipline the CCC became a natural boot camp for the approaching war. Few in our region, however, conceived it in that manner in the 1930s since they wished to avoid war at all costs.

We benefited the most from the WPA (Works Progress Administration) projects which existed from 1933 to 1943. The one with which I had the greatest familiarity was the straightening of Highway 63 for about a quarter of a mile north of Mammoth Spring, Arkansas. In 1935 the highway ran along a stream to the northeast corner of the lake that was created by damning the gigantic spring, then in a sharp curve turned west past the spring, then again sharply to the south toward the village. While guard cables prevented most vehicles from going over the embankment into the lake, through the years, on occasion, one ended up in the water. In about 1935 I was occasionally invited to go with my Uncle Cleo and Aunt Ova to visit her parents in Mammoth Spring. My uncle would put me on his lap and let me steer. I did well until we came to the sharp curves at the spring. My uncle would then grab the steering wheel. Aunt Ova tried to get him to put me back on the seat, but he argued that he could control the vehicle. WPA funds were requested and appropriated to straighten out the highway by making a cut through the bluff to the west of the spring. Additional fill was required, and the administrators of the project negotiated with my grandfather to remove a large stone fence to add to the roadbed from the property straight east of his grocery-gas station. The fence was about a quarter of a mile in length and was on both sides of the property line between grandfather's field and the farm to the south. Uncle Cleo had bought the farm to the south. The fence was in some places six feet across with rocks stacked three to four feet high though not consistently that large. The WPA brought a crew of about twenty men to load the stones by hand onto the dump trucks. Those who received checks from the WPA were unemployed prior to working. A crew foreman was a leader in the church at Mammoth Spring. It puzzled my relatives as to why he would work for the WPA, but they weren't too critical.

Our immediate family watched the rock-loading crews with interest because they were under the impression that WPA workers were lazy. The common jibe was that WPA stood for "We piddle around." They noticed that the workers received regular breaks, which did not happen on jobs in our area, and that bosses for the project did not do any of the manual labor.

The longest lasting project around Thayer was the building of drainage ditches, retaining walls, curbs, and sidewalks on several of the streets in town. These were WPA projects. The walls and curbs were all constructed with native stone, mostly sandstone, but sometimes flint. Such flat stones could be found in fields all over, though sand stones often had to be split, the accomplishment of such was easily achieved. The stones on the retaining-walls were separated with mortar, then a concrete bead highlighting each individual stone was mortared on. About a half mile of the sidewalk that I traveled daily to and from Thayer Elementary school was built on each side in this manner. I, therefore, observed the daily progress while going to and from school. Several men were involved in the work, but in smaller groups. What they did improved the drainage and looks of the street immeasurably. Some of these construction projects may still be seen though some repairs have been necessary down through the years.

The major project for our county was building the Oregon County Court House on the square in Alton in 1939—somewhat late in the program. The old courthouse was wood framed. The new court house was built of red granite mined in Ironton, Missouri, about two hundred miles northeast of Thayer near St. Louis. The county floated a bond issue for $25,000 and received a federal WPA grant for $75,000. I was under the impression that some of the construction was funded by the PWA, which employed skilled people who worked for a private company. WPA labor pay came directly from federal sources to the workers while PWA monies might be given to private contractors who paid the workers. Another local project built by the WPA was the "city" park at Mammoth Spring on the right-hand side of the highway to Salem. It was a nice large park with picnic tables, drinking water, and even a tennis court.

Missouri Memories, 1934–1947

MY TAYLOR GRANDPARENTS

When I was five in the summer of 1935, I started staying part of the summer with my grandparents. Uncle Wellington was home from college for the summer and he sometimes played with me. He was a student at Southwest Missouri Teacher's College, Springfield, now Missouri State University. For people who were entrepreneurs the Depression years were an excellent time to obtain college degrees. My Uncle Cleo who started to college a bit before the Depression took over a paper route for the *Springfield Daily News*. He expanded it and became supervisor of several routes. By the time he graduated from SMSTC he was making more money than he did from his first teaching job. Uncle Wellington also delivered papers but he was not as aggressive as his older brother, but did well. By the time I entered the third grade in 1937 I started staying with my grandparents, T. Shelt and Myrtle Taylor, year around. The Taylors lived a half mile south of my parents, and I often went home and spent a day or two. Glenn and Owen could take care of all the chores at home so my parents didn't mind. I preferred to stay clear of my brothers because they were noisy and wrestling all the time. My grandparents were glad for me to stay with them since there was always plenty to do. I helped pump gas and sell knick knacks and groceries. We literally pumped gas. The gas pumps had a ten gallon glass bowl on top with lines marked for the gallons. At the side of each pump was a handle about two and half feet long. In order to pump one stood at the side and pushed the handle back and forth parallel to the pump. In that manner the bowl above was filled. A rubber hose extended from the bottom of the tank with a nozzle on the end which when the trigger was released let the gas flow by gravity into the car tank. In the middle 1930s gasoline often sold for 9.9 cents a gallon. I recall one time in the midst of a gas war we sold regular for 7.9 cents.

My grandfather sometimes bought produce from truckers who came from another part of the region; one of his favorites was to buy a truckload of watermelons grown around Cave City, Arkansas. He bought a large load at the time of the Mammoth Spring Old Settler's Reunion since many persons attending the reunion drove by the station. He usually sold them for a quarter, but sometimes toward the end he dropped the price to ten cents a melon. When he had melons he typically called all those present at the house and station in the middle of the afternoon to eat melon. He would yell toward the house nearby, "Myrt, bring a knife." We had both red and yellow melons and loved both. Granddad only wanted to eat the hearts, normally the most succulent part of the melon. The remainder would go to the pigs who loved them. We often ate down to the rind, however. We ate the large slices in the yard with the juice dripping down our chin and would spit the seeds into the Bermuda grass. We normally had a cloth handkerchief with which we wiped our faces.

The Old Soldier's Reunion, which commenced in 1883 for former Civil War soldiers, was held on the northeast side of the dammed-up, 18-acre-Spring Lake. The reunion flourished during the Depression since about the only other entertainment was high school sports and picture shows as they were called then. A carnival consisting of rides, side shows, refreshments, and game booths set up a day before the reunion began. There was no admission charge, and the other costs were small. The game rides were a nickel in the daytime and a dime at night. Hamburgers or hotdogs were $.15. Many persons attended the reunion, especially families and teenagers. Older people came in the day time and visited with friends and relatives whom they mostly saw at the annual reunions. I normally got to go a time or two at night taken by one of my uncles. I loved the merry-go-round and cotton candy. I steered clear of the Ferris wheel because of severe motion sickness especially when coming down.

I learned many fine characteristics from my grandfather. He was always eager to attack whatever came up. In the summer we sat outside under the canopy over the gas pumps in metal chairs. My grandfather never waited until a car stopped to walk up to the driver. He was up as soon as he saw someone turn off the highway. In winter we sat inside behind a large picture window, and we were out the door by the time most people got out of their car. My grandfather was always warm in greeting people, even Blacks. He didn't think Blacks should live in Oregon County, and they didn't, but he believed they had a soul just like white people and should be treated accordingly. He preferred that the Blacks not use the rest rooms, but he didn't bar them. Often the men went down into the barn about fifty feet from the pumps.

My grandfather encouraged me to do whatever there was to do around the store and gas station and to learn as fast as I could. At the early age of six, I became intrigued with maps. I liked to travel, though I didn't often have the opportunity, and I liked to learn where people came from and where they were going. Grandfather often asked people where they lived. At that time most oil companies produced free maps of all the forty-eight states and sent them to the gas stations to distribute free. We didn't always have maps of all the 48 states, but we had many and especially all within 500 miles of our location. When we didn't have customers I often studied the maps. I soon memorized the numbers of the major highways around our area—for example, US 63, Missouri 19, US 60, along with the names of the various towns and the distances. My grandfather was proud of my knowledge. If we were inside and someone asked distances and directions, he would point to me and say, "Ask that seven-year-old boy over there." If they seemed willing to hear, I would tell them. If they looked skeptical I laid out a map and showed them. Granddad was always willing for me to ask questions whether he knew the answers or not.

My Uncle Norval was not of the same disposition. He and Aunt Mabel never had children, but Uncle Norval often took an interest in me and my brothers. Later, when Glenn and Owen were into high school sports Uncle Norval was foremost among their fans. Since I was the oldest, Uncle Norval tended to single me out in the Depression years. I sometimes spent a night with him and Aunt Mabel. Uncle Norval traveled the whole of Oregon County to deliver oil and gas to stations and large farms. He took me on a few short trips. One day we went to Billmore in the southeast corner of the county. I was of course thrilled since I hadn't been there before but I knew the territory on the maps. For about ten miles east of Thayer, I knew the names of all the streams, the owners of several farms and the small towns. On the way to Billmore when we got into the areas I didn't know I started asking my uncle for names, etc. Sometime he knew and sometimes he didn't. But after awhile he told me I asked too many questions. When he dropped me off back at my grandparents' he told my grandfather he would never take me again because I asked so many questions. And he was faithful to his word.

When Uncle Norval was drafted for World War II in 1942 Aunt Mabel lived by herself. She liked to attend movies and probably went at least once a week. When I was thirteen she started inviting me along. I especially liked the westerns. One time we went, and my cousin James Ray was there. He wanted me to sit with him, so I asked Aunt Mabel if that was all right and she reluctantly said "yes." I think it happened one more time. Aunt Mabel told my Aunt Alice that she wasn't going to invite me anymore because she expected me to sit with her. I was able to alienate both Uncle Norval and Aunt Mabel.

As I think back, I am somewhat surprised at the movie attendance in the middle thirties. It was usually good at matinees and sometimes a packed house at night. My dad never went to the movies. The only time I ever recall him going was about 1936 when his brother Frank and wife Minnie from Crawford, Nebraska, came to visit us and the other Olbricht relatives. Apparently they attended movies regularly. I recall the cartoon of Felix the Cat and a film starring Betty Boop. I don't remember the main feature. My mother sometimes went to matinees and took us kids along.

My grandfather never liked to travel far but he loved to go on short trips to visit churches or relatives. When I was about five, my grandfather heard an announcement that a Gospel meeting was being held at a Church of Christ in Williford, Arkansas. He wanted to go because the preacher's name was L. N. Moody, and grandpa's father was John Moody Taylor who was descended on his mother's side from the Moodys. Granddad thought we might be related to L. N. Moody. Uncle Wellington drove the pickup, I sat in the middle, and grandpa on the outside. In those days all the highways in Northern Arkansas were gravel. Moody was a fluent preacher, and I still recall his sermon in that small white clap board church building. He preached from the text, "So then because thou art lukewarm, and neither cold nor hot, I will spew thee out of my mouth," Rev 3:16 (KJV). The declaration was vivid and memorable. He preached a somewhat different sort of sermon and came down hard on those members who lacked dedication. A few seemed to be squirming. I don't think grandpa and L. N. Moody were able to pin down whether they were related.

Granddad, too, on occasion visited his brothers and sisters. The first time I recall going to Alton was with grandpa and grandma to visit his older brother Calvin. Calvin was retired and lived in a small house on the highway going east. Cal, as my grandfather called him, held an elected office as Oregon County Sheriff for several years. I remember how aged he and his wife looked as they sat in rocking chairs on the front porch and talked with my grandparents as the cars passed by. He often said that his biggest regret in life was being ordered to hang a man.

We also went to visit granddad's sister, Della James. The James had a farm on Janes Creek east of Wirth, Arkansas, about 20 miles southeast of Thayer. They lived in an old-style log house with the dining room and kitchen separated from the rest of the house by an open hallway. The reason for houses of this sort was that most house fires originated in the kitchen. In that manner, if the kitchen caught fire, the living quarters most likely could be saved. The house had a large dining room with a daisywheel table in the center. The table was six feet in diameter. The daisywheel in the middle was about five feet. All the food was placed on the daisywheel and one could turn the wheel to take off the desired items. I was intrigued by the daisywheel and turned it more than necessary until chided by my grandmother. Another intriguing feature of their house was that it was situated at the base of a hill. A spring was located at a distance some 200 feet higher than the house, and water was transported through a galvanized pipe from the spring to a large shallow metal tank at the southwest corner of the house. Since the water ran in and out, food items, especially milk products, were immersed in containers in the water to keep them cool. The pipe coming down the hill was elevated about a foot where it ran into the tank. Hanging nearby were a couple of gourd dippers. The gourds were a foot long with the ball part on the end about two inches in diameter. One filled the large cup end and drank it down with the water that was cool and refreshing. What a different sort of living style for this six year old!

ENTERTAINMENT

Even during the Depression several traveling entertainment groups came to town. The attendance was pretty good considering the Depression years. Most years a circus showed up and raised their tent at the Thayer Fairground northeast of Warm Fork Creek. The day the circus opened a man with a public address speaker on top of his car drove around town slowly blasting out information. My grandfather was not that interested in circuses so I don't recall going but perhaps a time or two and that likely with my class at school. Grandfather, however, was especially attracted by traveling "Toby" tent shows, and I recall going to perhaps three with him. These were vaudeville melodramatic type productions that likewise set up a tent on the fairgrounds. Toby was the lead character, always wore a bright red wig and often played a banjo in Tin Pan Alley type musical groups. What I recall most, however, was him playing rinky-dink piano tunes during the intermissions. I especially enjoyed this music, and I recall my favorite piece was "Whispering," a 1920s hit. Several companies traversed the Midwest and Southwest, and I'm not sure where home base was for those that visited Thayer. Medicine shows also came to town, but I only recall going to one. I don't think granddad was that interested.

My grandfather usually kept his gas station and store open at night until 8:00 P.M., but sometimes later in the summer, especially when fairs and reunions were going on. Normally, we didn't close for dinner. Grandpa

Later Depression Years

would go to the house to eat first while Uncle Wellington or one of the cousins minded the store. They would eat later. Even I sometimes filled in when I reached eight years old. In the winter grandpa had a coal furnace in the basement of the store. It had a floor grate for heating which was in the center of the room near the southern edge. Grandpa had a padded chair on the far side close enough to the grate so that he could put his feet over it. There were two or three other chairs around. Occasionally persons would stop in, purchase something, then sit in a chair and talk for awhile. During the middle 1930s one regular visitor was Ed Murray, an eccentric who lived on a small plot of ground on the hillside about a quarter-mile south from the station. He constructed small cement rooms of all shapes and sizes onto a central room with tin roofs for his dwelling. He professed his love for cement and reported that one time he put some in his biscuits but they were tough to chew. Ed sat around and "spun yarns" in my father's view, as well as most others.

Sometimes his yarns had to do with travels. He told of heading west through the Colorado Rockies in the late twenties. The roads were mostly unpaved, and cars didn't have brakes that would keep functioning all the way down long mountain slopes. A normal way of helping slow the auto was to attach a good-sized log to the rear of the car with a chain tied so that the log dug into the soil. He told of once going down a slope, but the log did not dig in as it should. The car kept speeding up, so as he described it he opened the door and "jined the bird gang," that is, he was airborne for a time before landing; none the worse except for a few scratches. Most of his stories had to do with business deals. He told of living in the state of Washington for a time where he bought property with trees suitable for logging. He kept it for a couple of years, built a shack on it, and sold it two years later for $1500 more than he paid for it. At that time $1500 was perhaps what an unskilled laborer could make in four years. I always listened attentively whereas my elders would drift in and out. At first they thought I was being taken in. One night after some long-winded tale with mention of much money changing hands and after Ed left, I said to my grandfather, "Ed sure made a lot of money tonight, didn't he?" My grandfather laughed and later told my parents, aunts and uncles.

Grandfather had a burglar alarm on the door and windows of the store, and the alarm sounded in his bedroom about a hundred fifty feet away. Since money was so scarce break-ins were rather common. Granddad slept with a loaded pistol on a table by his bed. I slept in a second floor bedroom overlooking the highway and I could see the driveway from the highway down to the store. Grandpa said he never wanted to kill or wound anyone, and in fact he wasn't a very good shot with the pistol. If the alarm went off he would run out the front door of the house, somewhat hidden from the store by porch pillars, and fire the pistol into the air. More than once I was awakened by hearing a shot then squealing tires as the thieves sped away. We would go down to the store and usually find signs of efforts to jimmy the door or a window. I don't recall that grandfather ever lost anything from within the store in those years, but sometimes used tires that were left outside were stolen.

After the attempted break-ins occurred, I often slept fitfully. We heard various stories about gangs roaming the country sometimes wounding or killing those they attempted to rob. I was afraid that grandpa, or even I, might be inflicted. A well known gang, the Ma Barker gang, actually rented a hideout not far from Thayer. The gang was made up of Ma and her sons—Herman, Lloyd, Arthur, and Fred. Also associated with them was Alvin "Creepy" Karpis. They left the region, however, after they killed the Howell County Sherriff, C. Roy Kelly, in late 1931. These stories did not encourage good sleeping for a preteen during the night when noises erupted from near the gas station.

At the end of the Depression, shortly before World War II, Uncle Wellington took a position as a vocational agriculture teacher in Ellington, Missouri, in the heart of Missouri pine logging country and in the Mark Twain National forest 70 miles northeast of Thayer. We went to visit Uncle Wellington and Aunt Dortha. As I recall Aunt Alice drove, grandpa rode up front with her and grandma and I sat in the back seat. It was about a two-hour drive up highway 19 through Alton and Winona, then across 60 to Van Buren and up 21 to Ellington. The roads were paved but very crooked. The old jibe Uncle Ted told me was that the engineers designing the highway were paid by the mile so they lengthened the highway by adding as many curves as possible. The truth, however, was that most of the terrain was quite hilly and the engineers sought to follow the contours of the land, requiring as few cuts and fills as possible. I was car sick most of the way up and vomited two or three times. On the way home I mostly slept. Despite the nausea I really enjoyed the trip. At Greer, a few miles northeast of Alton, the pine trees started growing. There were no pines in our region unless transplanted and those did not do well. It was thought that the soil was not suitable for pine. North of Van Buren beautiful tall pines bordered the highway, some of them virgin pines. By that time I was intrigued with sawmills and I envisioned the amazing pine logs that could be cut near Ellington. Most of my traveling in the Depression years was with my grandfather and sometimes my grandmother. They loved to travel. About 1938 my grandmother and Aunt Alice drove to Alto in east Texas to visit two of her Dunsmore brothers and families who had moved there some years previously.

UNCLE WELLINGTON AND SWIMMING

I got to see part of our region because of Uncle Wellington's venturesome nature. He liked to visit all the unusual places in the region, usually with a friend, and he sometimes took me along. Warm Fork Creek flooded periodically in the spring of the year. About 1935, a major flood developed following two days of constant rain. Uncle Wellington wanted to see the flooded creek. He, a friend of his, and I first traveled north to Thayer and down to the bridge going east. The water had come past the train depot and was about a foot deep in the waiting room. Only the bridge was visible. Below the on-ramps on either side of the bridge the water was so deep that it would likely be a day before a normal crossing could occur. We next drove toward Mammoth and around the north end of the spring. Large buildings there housed a wholesale grocery depot, a chicken processing plant and sometimes a cannery for blackberries, strawberries, and peaches. At that point going east was a low water bridge to Shelbyville which was adequate under normal conditions, but certainly not during a flood. It was not possible to get anywhere near the bridge. Above the bridge was a deeper pool where people swam called Shelby Hole, perhaps mostly utilized by high school boys. I recall one night about dark Uncle Wellington and a friend, perhaps Hilton Griffith, took me down to the swimming hole, as we called it, on a hot summer night, and we swam awhile before returning home. I don't recall when I first learned to swim. My father built a cement water storage pool about 12' by 12' southeast of the well house. We had a windmill on the well which, as long as the wind blew, kept the pool overflowing. The excess ran into the garden. The pool was about three feet deep. We started swimming in that pool perhaps as early as age two.

Another common place for swimming was the dammed-up Mammoth Spring Lake of eighteen acres. About 1937, the steel bridge across the lake was abandoned for auto use. It stood about 10 feet above the water.

The water in the lake was 20 feet deep, making it ideal for diving, either from the floor level or from the top of the steel frame which was about eight feet higher than the floor. Someone had attached a ladder to the side of the bridge, so we were able to climb out of the lake. The only difficulty was that the water was 58 degrees year around. It felt good, however, on a day when the temperature stood at 98 and the humidity almost at that percentage. The difficulty was getting accustomed to the cold. Most of us decided the best way was just to jump in and confront the cold all at once. It took our breath for a minute, but we stayed in a short time then climbed out. As long as we didn't dry off we were acclimatized and could continue diving, climbing out and diving in again. It was not until high school years that my brothers and I swam there without adult relatives present. My specialties were a cannon ball and a back flip, but I also did front flips and swan dives. A power house was near the dam on the lake and generated electricity and continued to do so until 1972. In the late 1960s the spring and the surrounding area was made into a state park, and the lake was lowered. Uncles Wellington, Cleo and others took us to the national fish hatchery established east of the spring in 1903. Fish were exhibited behind glass but also in perhaps two dozen shallow spawning pools surrounding the buildings. I especially liked to observe the large rainbow trout—around ten pounds—floating lazily around in the assigned pool. As I recall there was no admission charge to the hatchery.

Another place Uncle Wellington took me, and perhaps Nedra, was to the Grand Gulf west of Thayer about ten miles The gulf was caused by the collapse of a natural roof over an underground river. Such a formation was unusual in that it produced a gulf of about a mile long with side arms of some yards in length. The gulf lay about 150 feet deep below ground level. There was a natural bridge and a small stream at the bottom with several walking trails. The area became a Missouri State Park in 1984. We also traveled about 10 miles south to Many Islands, Arkansas, which was on the Spring River, created by the confluence of water from the spring and the Warm Folk branch of the river just below the dam at Mammoth. A few small camps were located along the river. One of my favorite spots was the Narrows located about 20 miles east of Thayer on the Eleven Point River. I had wanted to see it for a long time, so one Sunday afternoon Uncle Wellington took my brothers and me there. The Narrows is a high hog back ridge that separates Frederick Creek and the run off from Blue Springs from the Eleven Point River valley. The narrow ridge is about a half mile in length. What impressed me was seeing several large gar fish, sometimes called garpike, in the water, some almost three feet long.

Pools created in rivers by the natural water flow and by the shifting of sand and gravel were important swimming holes. Ozark streams, unless flooded were clear and appropriate for swimming. We had many places available for outdoor recreation and no admission fee was required. I have already mentioned Shelby Hole and the Mammoth Spring Lake. East of Thayer and north of the old fairground was a pool in the Warm Fork where I swam a few times with Jim Dunsmore and Jack Mainprize, but I was not often in that part of town. In 1945, it was used for baptizing by the Thayer Church of Christ. I was baptized there along with my two brothers and a cousin, Don Beatty. North of Thayer, on the way to Alton, was a pool to the east of where highway 19 crossed the Warm Fork, designated Mill Pond, because at one time a mill was located there. This pool had a feature common to several such southern Missouri swimming holes—a rope swing tied high on a tree that leaned over the hole. The rope was knotted several times at the end and served as a lump upon which to clamp one's legs. As one swung over the pool one could drop off feet first, dive head first, do a flip or a cannon ball. Our parents, however, ordered us not to use the swings because too many young persons had been killed by hitting their heads on rocks or through diving into shallow gravel. I swam there a few times with Uncle Cleo.

Our family's favorite pool was at Sloan Ford ten miles northwest of Thayer on the Warm Fork just beyond a low water bridge. We mostly went to Sloan Ford on the fourth of July. My dad didn't celebrate holidays much, but for some reason he always celebrated the fourth of July. Since we raised many chickens, mom would almost always fry chicken and pack it in a basket. We also had plenty of potatoes—so potato salad too. We also had bread and cookies. Before we left home my dad made a hand-turned ice cream freezer full of vanilla ice cream. We bought ice from the ice plant in Thayer; $.50 for a 50-pound block. Dad wrapped the freezer in two wet burlap bags, and it remained frozen until after we had swum a bit and eaten lunch. There wasn't much of a pool at Sloan Ford so we waded up and down the creek which normally was waist high. Dad sometimes waded with us when he was younger. There was a hill on the southwest side of the stream. In one area was a steep bank and somewhere above the bank was a small spring. The spring ran slowly over the bank which was covered with moss; toward the bottom it dripped and was designated "Dripping Springs." We were fascinated by the way the water flowed and would watch for several minutes.

Chapter V

Childhood Activities

During the Depression we had a number of pastimes that kept us busy. We were never without something to do. Mother supervised our play in the daytime when school was out. The field north of our house had all sorts of persimmons trees which were common throughout our region. Some trees were relatively young and grew in copses. Some were large, perhaps forty feet high. An especially large tree grew near the highway. It had limbs low to the ground which made it easy to climb. Near the top, the branches forked in such a manner that comfortable seats resulted. Nedra and I both loved to sit high above the ground and watch the cars whiz by and the people walking along the highway. Sometimes we yelled at them, catching them by surprise because they couldn't see us through the leaves.

We discovered in playing with neighborhood kids that if we cut a small persimmon branch about three feet long and sharpened one end so that a green persimmon could be pushed on it, then, with the flick of the wrist, we could launch the persimmon at a high velocity thirty feet or more. That was much fun. It was also fun to direct the persimmons at our playmates. If agile, they could duck, but once and awhile the persimmon hit their body or head producing a stinging pain. If a sibling got hit the likelihood was that he or she ran into the house crying. The result was that we were prohibited from throwing persimmons in that fashion at other people. So mother had to be more on guard against harmful activities than she really cared to be.

After school our neighbor to the south had a field sometimes used by adults for softball and baseball. We had a stile in our pasture near the ball field where we could climb over the fence with ease. Perhaps a half dozen neighborhood guys drifted in, usually to play football in the fall and softball in the spring and summer. Our parents preferred softball over baseball because they thought baseball was dangerous. We sometimes played marbles, and back at the house we played jacks on the front porch. After dark we played Chinese Checkers and Monopoly inside. My mother and granddad and grandmother Taylor loved to play Chinese Checkers. My grandmother was especially good at it and could win most every time. For some reason we didn't like checkers that much. Another diversion for me, especially after I started staying with my grandparents when I was in the third grade, was reading comic books. At that time new comics were appearing regularly. Superman, Batman, Spiderman and Wonder Woman were already in print and other comic book series were being released regularly. I stuck with the popular ones. Grandfather routinely went to the Thayer Barber Shop to be shaved by his nephew, Bynum Dunsmore, on Saturday Night about 8 P.M. and about once a month to get his hair cut. The truth was he loved to be shaved, but he attributed the habit to his desire to help out his nephew. I was permitted to go with him. As he waited and was shaved I went to the corner drugstore, ordered a chocolate malt, and normally picked out a comic book or two. I had my own money since granddad normally gave me a silver dollar a week for helping him. I started collecting comic books. I also traded them with my cousin James Ray Dunsmore. By the time I graduated from the eighth grade I had a stack of comic books almost three feet high. I had a wonderful collection, and if I still had them in good shape they would likely be worth a half a million dollars. Unfortunately, however, they were well read with some covers missing, dog eared, and sometimes torn. They still would have a value, however. When I went to college I told my parents to do whatever they wanted to do with them. They weren't worth much at that time. They either gave them away or burned them.

Uncle Wellington created an interesting diversion for us. When Uncle Cleo started wintering cattle at grandpa's we fed them hay along with silage. For awhile he bought prairie hay in railway car load lots from southeast Missouri. We unloaded the hay—often late at night—up into the hayloft of granddad's barn. Later we stacked baled alfalfa hay grown on the farm. All this hay was in bales about 1 X 1.6 X 3 feet. Uncle Wellington, with our help, restacked the bales so we had a cave in the middle of the hay loft about 6 X 8 X 6 feet. The ceiling of the cave was held up by boards with bales stacked at least two deep on top. The entrance to the cave through a tunnel was hidden and required crawling down a six-foot passageway. That was our hiding place. We sometimes took a flashlight. Lighting a match was obviously forbidden. We mostly relished the secrecy of our cave and did boy talk.

FISHING

When I was five or six, on occasion, I fished for catfish in farm ponds at grandpa Olbrichts or at Uncle Ernest's. I can't say, however, that I caught the fishing bug right away. One time in the middle thirties Uncle Ernest Sauser, my father's step-brother, and his wife Pearl, who was a double cousin of my mother, invited several relatives for a fish fry. To the north of their farmstead was a large pond about 100 feet in diameter. It was not too deep. It may have resulted from an old shallow sink hole. Some thought that it was hollowed out more because it had become a salt lick for deer. Small catfish grew prolifically in it. On the day of the fish fry three or four of the men waded through the pond with a seine and in two or three runs caught as many fish as needed. They picked out the largest ones that weighed about a pound. We ate fried catfish and cornbread along with green beans. Various apples had ripened, and the Sausers had a small hand turned cider press. We kids made all the fresh apple juice we could drink. The Sausers had gone into growing apples in a big way. They had about 80 acres of trees. Apples did well in our region, though sometimes the early blossoms were surprised by frost. Uncle Ernest had one of the few commercial orchards.

By the time I was ten, I became enamored with fishing in a major way, having heard fishing stories from cousins and others. My dad never went fishing nor did my uncles. There were no fishing poles to borrow. Since my dad would never consider money for fishing equipment, and I preferred to spend my own money for malts and comic books, I had to improvise. Numerous sassafras trees grew in copses throughout our region. In the middle of the copse the trees grew straight and tall. Sassafras was light, yet a fairly strong wood. My brothers and I took a hatchet and cut down three small trees. Out of each we created a pole about 10 feet long. I bought a small fishing kit at the Benjamin Franklin Five and Ten in downtown Thayer that consisted of line, hooks, floats and sinkers. My brothers and I equipped three fishing poles from the acquired equipment. We knew that fish tended to bite shortly after dawn, so with our parents' permission we left home at five A.M. on a fine summer day and walked a mile east to Warm Fork Creek where we had seen people catch fish. We located a likely spot and threw in our lines. For bait we had dug worms in the garden where mom threw the table scraps into what now would be designated a compost pile. We began to get bites immediately. How thrilling! We were catching blue gills about the size of an adult's hand. In over an hour's time we caught five. By the time the sun was high enough to cast beams over the pool, the fish quit biting. We took our string and headed home. Mom was pleased and helped us dress the fish which later she fried.

For some reason we did not continue to fish in the Warm Fork. We rather fished in Cox Creek. Cox Creek was on the other side of the Warm Fork and ran into it from the east. It was a fairly large stream and ran most of the year since it was spring fed. It ran through the Ray Dell farm on which was located an excellent spring. The spring had a fence around it to keep the cattle out. Ray Dell was a traveling dry goods salesman and did pretty well even in the Depression years. He had identical twin daughters my age, Mary Lou and Alice Sue who were usually in my classroom at school. They were cute. Many people couldn't tell them apart, but I learned how rather quickly through the greater vivaciousness of Alice Sue. We normally played in the waters of Cox Creek near the Dell spring. In the spring of the year the creek was inhabited by sunfish; some were sizable for the species. As the summer wore on, the water diminished, and it was possible for us to pull these red gills out of crevices under the bank with our hands. As we grubbed we sometimes felt snakes. The snakes may have been Water Moccasin or Cottonmouth, both highly poisonous species. We held the "old wives' view" that if they bit underwater we wouldn't be poisoned. Fortunately, we never got bit, and we were usually able to take a few sunfish home for Mom to fry. We attached them to a long cord called a stringer and kept them in the water until we were ready to go home.

Richard Martin, one of my classmates, was always fishing. His parents ran a pharmacy downtown Thayer and lived not far from the Warm Fork. Along the way he acquired the nickname "fish face" Martin. He was in his element when the yellow suckers ran upstream in the spring. It was possible from the Warm Fork Bridge to easily spot the suckers in the water below. Suckers were long and somewhat narrow, the larger ones weighing up to two pounds. Richard mastered the art of grappling suckers from the bridge. A grapple hook consisted of three large attached prongs curled up and tied to a strong line at the end of a rigid fishing pole. The grappling technique was to drag the triple hook along the bottom upstream toward the bridge, come up under a school of suckers, then jerk quickly in hopes of hooking a fish. A good time of day was lunchtime since the fish could be seen clearly in the bright sun. We had an hour for lunch at school so two or three times I ran with Richard down to the creek about a half mile away and watched him grapple. In the course of fifteen minutes he might hook a half a dozen suckers. He would drop them off at his house and we would race back up the hill so we wouldn't be late for class. He let me grapple a time or two but I don't think I ever grabbed a sucker.

VISITING

My parents were rather free to let me stay with relatives overnight or longer. By the time I was eight, I had spent several nights with my grandparents, a night or more with Uncle Norval and Aunt Mabel, and a time or two with Uncle Cleo and Aunt Ova. I occasionally stayed overnight with Bynum and Opal Dunsmore. Their son James Ray was a year younger than I. We both loved comic books. I learned—though not well—to ride his bicycle because my father didn't want us to have one.

At around age seven, I was invited to spend a few days with Rob Hicks, with whom my father worked, and his wife Stella. They had older daughters and a son Lewis who was two years older than I. Rob was a nephew of my grandmother and Stella was a niece of my grandfather. Stella was a pleasant outgoing person who liked to talk with kids. I don't recall too much about that visit, but I do remember following Lewis around through the gardens, planted fields, and woods until the inner parts of my thighs were badly chafed My mother made my underwear from flower sack material and it was rather rough. I wore bibbed overalls, even to school when I was younger, which were made out of coarse material. The remedy I was given by Stella was rubbing alcohol. When first applied it stung sharply, but after the initial burning, it soothed the chaffing. Rob made furniture when not occupied building structures, and I recall a wooden framed bed that was something of a loft where Lewis and I slept.

We visited Uncle Ernest and Aunt Pearl Sauser occasionally. The Sausers lived on a farm and were developing, as I have already reported, a major apple orchard. They had an older daughter Evelyn, a younger daughter Grace, and a son Walter, two years older than I. The Sauser children attended a one room school at Rose Hill seven miles east of Thayer. They started school about the middle of August and then recessed a month in October so that students could help pick cotton on their own farms or that of others. Cotton was grown to the east and south of the Sauser farm on flat fertile fields along the rivers and designated river bottom farms. Nedra and I were invited to spend a week with them before our school started in Thayer. We walked to school with them daily on a path through their farm and other farms for about a mile and a half. Students at Rose Hill were permitted to go barefoot which was not the case in Thayer. I loved to go barefoot and did most of the summer, so that was fine, but sections of the path possessed protruded rocks so that we had to be careful not to stub a toe.

The Sauser cousins attended a one room school which I found fascinating. The various age groups sat in different corners, and the teacher worked with each group in succession. When not being instructed by the teacher the students either read or wrote in workbooks. Since I had no responsibilities I mostly listened to what was happening to each group as the teacher worked with them.

Walter and I played some after school, but he had various farm chores; I helped him. He was a fun loving person and somewhat mischievous. I think his mother somewhat relished those traits, but not his father. Uncle Ernest's father died when he was two years old. His mother married my grandfather two years later. My grandfather was distant to children and fairly stern, but Uncle Ernest was even sterner. He was known as a man of few words, but a hard worker. He set out to restrain Walter's exuberance. We completed the chores, but played along the way. The barnyard contained two stacks of straw about ten feet high recently brought in from the fields. It was great fun climbing to the top, then sliding down. The only problem was that as we slid so did some of the straw, bunching up at the bottom. Walter had been warned more than once about sliding down the stacks. He couldn't resist, however, and we had fun for perhaps a half hour climbing and sliding. Uncle Ernest was out in the orchards working. When he returned to the house for supper and looked around he saw the straw at the bottom of the stacks; he called loudly, "Walter." We knew that we or at least Walter was in trouble. Uncle Ernest told Walter to go get the razor strap. When Walter returned he told him to bend over. He hit him hard across the seat three or four times. I'm sure it stung, but Walter took it like a man. I thought for sure I might get it too, but it was uncommon for parents to discipline other people's children. I was relieved, but still conscience struck even though I was spared the strap.

Childhood Activities

Uncle Wellington married Aunt Dortha in 1940. I was around Uncle Wellington when he commenced dating Dortha, so I heard him discuss her with his friends, and got to know her too before they married. I was shocked one night to discover that Uncle Wellington smoked regularly. He lighted up a cigarette as he and Aunt Dortha sat by a large brush pile we were burning on the Price place. All my close relatives were dead set against smoking. Uncle Wellington never smoked in the presence of his parents and tried to disguise his breath by chewing Juicy Fruit gum. The smell of that combination turned me off to Juicy Fruit.

Uncle Wellington and Aunt Dortha married in September of 1940 at the time my Great-grandmother Dunsmore died. I do not recall any church weddings in Churches of Christ at that time. Most weddings took place in homes or before a justice of peace. Since Dortha was from Howell County they were married in the home of Judge W. B. Hodges of West Plains, MO, a friend of her father. Two of Dortha's sisters were present, Mabel Hunter and Gladys Davis, along with Ben Hunter as witnesses as well as Mrs. Hodges. It was fortunate in a way that these were the plans since it did not detract from the funeral days for grandmother Dunsmore. Uncle Wellington and Aunt Dortha first moved to Ellington, MO, in 1941, where he took a position as a vocational agriculture teacher. But in 1942, a position came open in Summerville, MO, which was closer and much more convenient for visiting her parents and his.

In the summer of 1942, when I was twelve, I was invited to spend a week with them in their new rental house. I rode with them from Thayer, and it was understood that I would take the bus back to Thayer. We saw busses pass my grandfather's gas station all the time, but I had not been on one. I wanted very much to go but I was a bit fearful of riding the bus, because I would have to transfer from one bus to another in West Plains on the way back to Thayer.

I had a good week. I went with Uncle Wellington to his high school shop a day or two and watched him make things. Some of the time I stayed with Aunt Dortha and read or played games. One memorable experience for me was when we went to see a movie at Mountain View, MO, a larger town to the south. I only attended a few picture shows so this was a real treat. The movie, for some reason yet very vivid to me, was "Come Live with Me" starring Jimmy Stewart and Hedy Lamarr. I still recall the scene in which they were close to making a marriage commitment. They stayed in a room separated by a high screen. In the night they woke up, started talking and decided they were in love. They each climbed on a chair and with heads just above the screen, kissed for the first time. I was a bit titillated as we departed, but I soon dropped off to sleep and slept most of the way back to Summerville.

To get to Summerville one crossed the Jacks Fork River which ran through a beautiful, but rugged canyon. It was a great week and I wished I could stay longer, but it was time to go home. Uncle Wellington and Aunt Dortha put me on the bus and made sure I knew how to transfer. The bus stopped various places along the way, so I was fearful that I might get off before we arrived in West Plains. I also had to worry about finding a bathroom since there was none on the bus. I was even more wary of transferring in West Plains, but I made it. As I recall the bus let me off across from granddad's gas station, a courtesy common in that time.

DINING

Two of my aunts were vocational economic teachers—Aunts Bertha and Alice. They both cooked on occasion at my grandparents when I stayed with them. Aunt Alice lived with my grandparents until my great-grand mother died in 1940 then she lived with her first cousin, Margaret Gingerich, an elementary school teacher, in grandma's house. In the Depression years Aunt Alice sometimes invited people to dinner at grandma Taylor's and the meal would be served there. She tried to serve foods that were both nutritious and inexpensive. Aunt Alice's specialty was spinach mixed with heavy cream and baked in a large flat casserole dish with eggs baked in pockets in the spinach located over an inch from each other. Another delectable meal to me was large canned oysters fried in finely crushed cracker crumbs mixed in an egg batter. The third was a dessert of canned Alberta peaches folded into whipped cream. One time I went into the kitchen after dinner and the guests had left. I discovered that several peaches were uneaten so I probably ate four or five. After awhile I began to get nauseated and I ran out into the yard as soon as possible and vomited. That experience somewhat dampened my appetite for peaches and cream. I recall especially the above three items she prepared that appealed to me.

My mother loved greens of all sorts. So did I, which was rather unusual among my peers. Greens were obviously inexpensive to us because we could pick dock and sometimes even New Zealand spinach along the

Childhood Activities

roads, dandelions from our yard, various sorts of spinach and asparagus from our garden, and polk salad from the fringes of the woods.

Sometimes grandma traveled with Aunt Alice to visit relatives, and grandpa and I remained at the station. I learned to love his canned lunches, often sardines and crackers, but sometimes Vienna sausages. Once in awhile we would warm up a can of hot tamales or a cellophane-wrapped brick of chili con carne. Our lunches were inexpensive and quick even if not the most balanced.

RADIO

Speaking of grandfather, he loved listening to the radio. Uncle Wellington bought a small speaker and ran a wire from the house to the station so that the Philo console in the living room could also be heard down at the station, especially the news over KWTO (Keep Watching the Ozarks) Springfield, MO. Without fail, my grandfather would make it to the house by 8 PM on Saturday for the start of the Grand Ole Opry, broadcast on Station WSM from Nashville, TN. The program lasted until midnight. I was permitted to stay up until it was over, but I seldom lasted that long. Grandpa particularly loved to hear the monologues of Minnie Pearl. I learned to mimic her beginning phrase: "Howdy! I'm so proud to be here and just so glad I came." I also learned to sing the "Wabash Cannonball" in the manner of Roy Acuff. On many nights we could receive the Carter family from a clear channel 250,000 Watt station, XERA, Ciudad Acuña, Mexico, just across the border from Laredo, Texas. Stations in the United States were limited to 50,000 Watts. I learned to sing the Carter Family theme song, "Keep on the sunny side, always on the sunny side. Keep on the sunny side of life. It will help us every day, it will brighten all away if we'll keep on the sunny side of life." On week nights we listened to Amos and Andy. Grandpa especially loved their humor. In the 1930s the show was nightly. He also loved Jack Benny and Fibber McGee and Molly, whose closet always erupted when he opened the door. Radio prospered in the Depression. It was free to the consumer and a great advertising media.

FRIENDS

My close friends were Glenn and Owen, my brothers, James Ray Dunsmore, our cousin, and later Jack Mainprize in my class at school.

I also developed a short-term friendship in the second grade with Forrest Daller who lived just west of Highway 63 bypass about a third of a mile north of where we lived. I often walked home with him. Sometimes I would stay for a while at his house, and at other times he continued home with me to play. He was a good friend. We shared many interests. We were beginning to notice girls. One day he told me that he liked a certain girl, but that I was not to tell anyone. At that age playmates taunted others who seemed to pair off. I kept the secret for about a week; but one day I was involved with a group who were spouting off about which boy liked what girl and vice versa. I had a hard time containing Forrest's confidential confession, and finally blurted it out. In a day or two it got back to Forrest because someone regaled him with it. Forrest came to me and asked me if I told. I said I had. With a bit of anger in his voice, he said we could no longer be friends. I thought it was not really a serious matter and would blow over. But Forrest was true to his word. Regardless of what I did to make amends he rejected my friendship. A year or two later his family moved from Thayer.

I was the real loser. I lost a true friend. I learned the hard way from this experience the need to keep information confidential, both when charged, and for the most part, without being charged. Being a revealer of secrets is destructive to friendships. Sometimes one can develop friends among those who thrive on the latest gossip. But these people are never good friends over the long haul since they, in turn, gossip about you.

Jack Mainprize and I became close friends in the third grade. We loved to pass notes in class, which was forbidden by all the teachers. We were mostly given to passing notes regarding what we considered as clever observations of all that went on. The trick was to pass the note when the teacher's back was turned. Jack and I were usually separated so we had to pass to a seatmate who passed it on. One time we just made it when the teacher turned around. I had to pass the note to the girl behind me. So my arm would not be seen in motion I kept my hand on the back of my desk toward the girl. For some reason she started squirming. Seeing where my hand was, the teacher thought I was trying to reach for her leg. I was in trouble regardless, so I took my punishment which, as I recall, was staying after school a few days for an extra hour. The problem with this was I had to explain to my mother why I was late. In this case I think I got away with it by saying that I dilly dallied on the way home.

When I was in the fourth grade my mother's double cousin, Roy Dunsmore, was county superintendent—an elected office. Roy made at least annual visits to the various schools. One day he visited our school and sat in my history class taught by Bill Thomas, the elementary school principal. As the class ended Roy walked up the aisle where I sat and pulled a note off my back that said, "kick me." That was a common trick of lads our age. Jack Mainprize had put it there. Roy said, "Thomas do you really want to be kicked?" Embarrassed, I mumbled, "No." He spoke a few words to Bill the teacher but I don't think that Jack got into trouble. Jack tended not to get into trouble with the teachers since his father, a businessman, was chairman of the school board.

One of the honors for a fifth grade lad was to be nominated and appointed to the school boy patrol. We then served a year in the sixth grade. We were given a coat with a white belt diagonally across it so we could be easily seen. Our assignment was to stand at the edge of the street and escort younger students across to the school yard and back. We were instructed to hold up our hand to stop the cars. It was a rather heady responsibility at that age. Jack Mainprize was appointed captain and I a lieutenant. At another time of the day another classmate served as lieutenant. For some reason Jack did not like Paul Dubois, the other lieutenant, and wanted him out of the patrol. Jack talked with me about it and told me he was going to resign if Paul wasn't removed and asked me to resign with him. I was reluctant since I was pleased, and my Aunt Alice and my parents were proud. I liked serving at the crossings. I was ambivalent about resigning and hesitated. Jack kept pressuring me until finally I told him I would resign. I had explaining to do to my mother and Aunt Alice and didn't feel good about it, but I made it clear I did it for friendship. They did not approve the reason. But the resignation could not be revoked, and I was conflicted whenever I saw the patrols at work.

When I was in the seventh grade the state enacted a program to periodically weigh and measure the students. I think it was just the seventh graders, but it may have been all grades. I was always proud of my height and stood as tall as possible. I was the tallest person in our class. I was not so proud of my weight, however. I liked candy too much and could eat as much as I liked at grandfather's store. My dad got after me but I had trouble resisting. We weighed on a grocery store type scale placed in front of the class. When my time came, the scales and floor squeaked. Jack Mainprize let out a big laugh. Edward Kamm, our teacher, had been looking at the scale arm which registered 170 pounds and not at me. I was fully embarrassed. The last thing I wanted to do was call attention to my weight, but

Kamm accused me of deliberately squeaking the scales to cause people to laugh. I don't think Kamm would have suspected anything had Jack not laughed. In some ways with a friend like Jack who needed enemies? By the eighth grade we drifted apart.

In the late thirties economic conditions had improved. Uncle Cleo now had an increasing number of beef cattle on grandfather's farm and the contiguous acreage he had purchased. He had learned about atlas sargo and wanted to grow it for silage to feed cattle in the winter. He would also bring cattle down from Alton. It was up to Albert Prewitt and me to do the feeding. Albert was eight years older than I, and though we were third cousins, he became, in effect, my older brother.

The school year of 1940–41 was an exciting time. That summer my Uncle Cleo had a trench silo dug on the hill to the southeast above T. Shelt Taylor's gas station. Two or three years before, Uncle Cleo had purchased 50 acres from the Price estate on that hill. The trench silo was 150 feet long, ten feet wide, and five feet deep. We filled it with atlas sargo grown on the bottom land on T. Shelt's acreage east of the store. The crop was harvested after school began. We hauled it up the hill on pickups. A portable silage grinder was located at the silo and we filled the trench with chopped Sargo. We then covered the silage with a layer of straw and three inches of dirt.

My grandfather bought a 1934 Model B Ford pickup for us to drive around the farm. I learned to drive at age 11 in the Model B under the tutelage of Albert. One day Albert and I were in a field erecting a wire fence. We needed to move the pickup ahead, so without any instruction Albert told me to get in the pickup and pull it up. I had been sitting on uncles' laps for some time steering vehicles, and I knew how to start the pickup, engage the clutch, and put it in gear with the long stick shift extending from the floor. I also knew to press down on the gas pedal. But I had never given stopping much thought. I took off slowly, but when it came time to stop I didn't know what to do. I wasn't in much danger of hitting anything, but if I went too far I would go into the ditch at the back of the field. I somewhat panicked. Albert yelled for me to hit the brake. I pushed as hard as I could and fortunately killed the motor. Albert then gave me a few instructions on how to push in the clutch, hit the brake, and turn off the switch.

Albert went to Thayer High, I to Thayer Elementary. We sometimes rode to school with Aunt Alice who taught home economics and had her own car. That winter after school was out, Albert and I fed silage to the herd of beef cattle numbering thirty or so. We changed from our school clothes,

Childhood Activities

got in the pickup, and drove down the lane in the field and up the hill to the silo. We backed the pickup into the trench and up against the silage. Using digging forks we loaded the silage onto the pickup. We wore rubber boots because the silage was somewhat damp. The silage had a pungent pickled smell, indelibly fixed in my olfactory nerves even to this day. Down the hill from the silo were feed troughs into which we forked the silage for the cows. They crowded around, eating as we shoveled—trying to nudge us aside.

The winter of 1940–1941 was more severe than usual for southern Missouri. Shortly before Christmas the temperature dropped to 24 below on granddad's large Standard Oil thermometer situated on the north side of the station. In January snow fell a day or two, accumulating a foot or more and lasting for three weeks as the result of the accompanying cold temperatures. I loved snow for sledding. We had a small sled and there was one at grandpa's that belonged to Uncle Wellington (Tom) Taylor (1917–1993). Because the snow made it difficult for us to drive the pickup to the top of the hill, we had to start accelerating at the bottom so we could make it to the top. More than once we had to back down and start up again. Sometimes one of us would drive and the other would push. Albert would drive and I would push. If that didn't work he would have me drive and he would push. As I recall we always made it to the top, but a time or two with difficulty.

Because we drove up and down the hill the snow was packed and excellent for sledding. After a bit of melting in the daytime, toward nightfall the freeze sat in again. I recall under these circumstances sliding all the way from the top of the hill through the gate going into granddad's pasture on level ground. What a long ride—almost a quarter of a mile!

I loved those days. We worked hard. Forking and shoveling silage is hard work and my side sometimes hurt. Once in awhile I wanted to stop, but Albert always encouraged me, saying we were about done. Sometimes if I wanted to quit early on, he would shame me for being a "sissy." He told me of chopping cotton on their Janes Creek farm when he was my age. Chopping cotton was not only hard work, one was bent over the hoe much of the time. Furthermore, it was frequently hot in July and August. But the cotton had to be chopped, that is, the weeds removed. So I envisioned Albert's hardship and started pitching silage again, half way eager to prove I was a man!

We are who we are because of what we have shared with others. Albert's friendship and encouragement has loomed large in memory through the years. We not only worked together, we slept together in a double bed in the second story bedroom of my grandparent's native stone rock house on the side facing Highway 63 which ran from Thayer to Mammoth. It had a metal roof and sleeping as the rainstorms pelted down was wonderful. When the going got rough at various times in later life I recalled how Albert and I stuck it out and got the job done. With these fond memories etched in the back of my mind I finished many a difficult task. So farewell Albert Prewitt of fond memories! Though dead, through those of us who survive, you live on.

REFLECTIONS

I have thought much about the Depression years as I experienced them. I have read journals of others who lived through those years. It is commonplace to depict those times as difficult, depressing and debilitating. Who would long to struggle through such days? Some people just contemplating this extended, penny-pinching epoch can become extraordinarily depressed.

We, however, had many things to do and so much to see that I never really felt deprived. I would have loved to have had a bicycle, but I didn't have the best of places to ride it. There were always comic books, paths through the woods, playing in the ditches, building dams, playing football, shooting hoops, tossing a baseball, going swimming, playing Monopoly, and even playing a bit of golf on the nine-hole course on my grandfather's cow pasture.

Most of the adults I knew managed to have money for whatever they desired. In fact, my father thrived in the Depression economy because he believed in frugality, and such parsimoniousness was both required and admired in those years. Needed items cost little which enabled my father to add slowly to what he had accumulated over the years prior to the Depression and to see all his four children graduate from college in the post-war years. In part, we were able to work and pay for our own college expenses. I perceived that my Wisconsin father-in-law, Orville Kiel, approached the Depression with much the same outlook. In the 1980s I got to know Donald Hall, more recently United States poet laureate. He spent summers with his grandparents who flourished in the Depression climate in central New Hampshire. One of the books Hall wrote highlighting the thriftiness of his grandparents was titled, *String to Short to be Saved*. After his grandparents

Childhood Activities

died he told of finding a shoe box in the attic of their house with a label "string too short to be saved" filled with short pieces of twine. In the time and place as I look back I would not wish for a better upbringing than in those Ozark Depression years.

Chapter VI

My Religious Upbringing

Church involvement was very important in my more immediate extended family.

My earliest memories are of waking up during a night church service at the Centertown Church of Christ between Thayer, Missouri, and Mammoth Spring, Arkansas. I was perhaps three. I had gone to sleep on a simple bench with perhaps my head on my father's lap. I loved it when we sang, but the preachers tended to put me to sleep. Since I am something of an authority on Churches of Christ history I will set out information that will provide an adequate backdrop for appreciating my early church involvement.[1]

My father's parents were German Catholics, but I never knew my grandmother, who died when my father was four years old. My grandfather remarried, the second time to a German Lutheran. My mother's father grew up among American Restorationists, more recently identified as the Stone-Campbell Movement, and his wife came from Methodist backgrounds. My maternal grandmother was baptized as a Restorationist when she married my grandfather. A Restorationist preacher, that is, a Church of Christ preacher (G. K. Wallace), baptized my father when I was eight years old. He had been going to church with my mother from the time of my earliest memories. My principle religious roots are therefore Churches of Christ.

My paternal grandfather was born Heinrich Olbricht in Glatz, Germany (now Klodzko, Poland) in 1856. He was sprinkled at the local Roman

---

1. Olbricht, "Churches of Christ," Blowers, et al., *Encyclopedia*.

My Religious Upbringing

Catholic Church as an infant. The region where he was born in southeast Silesia was Roman Catholic. By age twenty my grandfather was apprenticed as a tanner, and traveled in Europe for two years, picking up jobs tanning as he went. He decided to migrate to the United States in 1878 where two of his brothers preceded him. There he met Katherine Eich, born in Bavarian Regensburg, Germany, also a Catholic region. In their early years of marriage they lived among German relatives in Elizabeth, New Jersey. Several Germans came to America before the Revolutionary War. The largest number of Germans settled in Pennsylvania. They were Lutherans and German Reformed. After the Civil War, Germans immigrated to America from farther east and were more likely to be Roman Catholic. They mostly settled in eastern cities, but later moved to Chicago and Milwaukee, and westward on farms in the upper Midwest.

My father, Benjamin J. Olbricht, was born in 1885. When my father's mother died my grandfather moved to western Nebraska in 1892 to homestead. His older brother Joseph preceded him to Nebraska. My father and siblings were taken to Nebraska a year later, and my grandfather later remarried, this time a German woman born in Russia/Poland—Bertha Lange Sauser. She was of German descent and a widow, and was the sister of my grandfather's brother Joseph Olbricht. Russian Tsars had encouraged Germans to colonize in regions of Russia. They were mostly Lutherans. In western Nebraska my grandparents lived almost twenty miles from the nearest town and therefore seldom attended church. In 1910 they bought a farm in Southern Missouri. There was a small Catholic Church in Thayer, and a small Lutheran church in the area, but again they did not attend much because they lived ten miles from town on rocky roads. I knew very little about their religious beliefs because we did not visit them much. I was never taken to a gathering of either a Catholic or a Lutheran Church.

My mother's father, T. Shelt Taylor, was born in Couch, Missouri, in 1876. His parents, John Moody Taylor (b. 1829) and Amy Anthum Waits Taylor (b. 1837) were born in Northwest Alabama. John Taylor served in the Confederate Army in the Civil War. At the end of the war he and his wife came under the influence of Restorationist preaching in the region, hearing a famous evangelist, T. B. Larimore preach shortly after the Civil War. By this time many Baptists in the region were converted to Restorationist principles by preachers from Tennessee, including Tolbert Fanning and David Lipscomb.

The Restoration churches (The Stone-Campbell Movement) began as independent groups in (1) Virginia, (2) New England, (3) Kentucky and (4) Pennslyvania—West Virginia—Ohio. In Virginia in the 1780s, a group of Methodist ministers led by James O'Kelly (1757–1826) sought freedom from supervision so that Methodist circuit riders could determine their own itinerary. Those who favored self-determinacy broke away, founding the Republican Methodist Church. In 1794 they changed the name of their congregations to the Christian Church. In New Hampshire and Vermont, persons of Baptist heritage, chiefly Abner Jones (1772–1841) and Elias Smith (1769–1846), formed new churches taking the name Christian only. The Bible was heralded, especially the New Testament, as the only source of authority and faith.

The two most important tributaries to the larger Restoration movement resulted from the work of Barton W. Stone (1772–1844) and the two Campbells, Thomas (1763–1854) and Alexander (1788–1866)—father and son. At the turn of the century the second Great Awakening titillated the Kentucky and Ohio frontiers. Five ministers among the Presbyterians, including Barton W. Stone, formed an independent presbytery. Not too long after, carrying their interests to their logical conclusions, they dissolved the Springfield Presbytery in order to "sink into union with the body of Christ at large." They identified themselves as Christian Churches. In 1807 Thomas Campbell, born in North Ireland of Scottish descent, arrived in Pennsylvania, settling in Washington County. Long a Presbyterian minister, he exerted considerable energy in the land of his nativity in a struggle to unify dissident Presbyterian groups. His efforts at similar rapprochement in Pennsylvania resulted in litigation to oust him from his presbytery. In 1809, his gifted son Alexander arrived with the rest of Thomas' family. Out of the Campbell's' efforts, churches were formed in the region around Pittsburgh. After 1816, the Campbells joined with Baptist ministers of the Redstone and later the Mahoning Associations, winning several Ohio and Kentucky Baptist churches to their outlooks. Early in the 1830s the churches from the Stone and Campbell groups commenced merging in Kentucky. The amalgamation expanded to churches in Pennsylvania, Ohio, Virginia, Tennessee, Indiana, Illinois, and Missouri. By 1850 Alexander Campbell, because of his journal editing, book publishing, debating, lecturing, and founding of Bethany College, became the best known leader of the movement.

By the time my great grandparents heard the Restorationist preachers and were baptized in Alabama in the 1860s there were many Restorationist

My Religious Upbringing

churches south of Nashville, Tennessee, and in northern Alabama. In 1869 my great-grandparents moved from northern Alabama, first to Southern Missouri east of Thayer, and later to Arkansas in 1880, a few miles south of the Missouri state line. They found Restorationist churches in this region and soon were at work among them. Restorationist preachers had come into the region as early as 1815 from the Stone movement in Tennessee/Kentucky. By the 1830s Baptists who had been influenced by Alexander Campbell moved into the region from Kentucky. In the 1840s a preacher named Daniel Rose from York, Maine, who had been ordained by Jones/Smith preachers, moved into the area.

My Great-grandfather and his family, including my grandfather T. Shelt Taylor, were active members in a Restorationist congregation called English Bluff southeast of Thayer, MO in Arkansas. When my grandfather was married in 1896 he too was an active leader in this congregation. My grandfather and grandmother Myrtle Dunsmore Taylor were baptized at the same time in 1896 by a preacher named Bynum Black. She was born in Ionia, Michigan, to a family of Methodists. The Methodists at that time were the largest religious group in America, except for the Roman Catholics. But I never visited the Methodist churches in our region and didn't know much about their beliefs. Several descendents of my grandmother's sister—Martha "Mattie" Dunsmore Green, were highly involved in an Assembly of God Pentecostal church. We lived near several members of that family and visited their church a time or two. We decided that the yelling of the preachers and members falling to the floor were exceedingly strange. Many Pentecostals came from Methodist backgrounds.

My mother, Agnes Taylor Olbricht (1898–1978), was baptized by a Restorationist preacher in the 1910s. By that time a division had occurred among the Restorationist churches creating the Christian Churches or Disciples of Christ, and the Churches of Christ. The division was reported in the 1906 Federal Census. Most of the Restorationists in our region went with Churches of Christ, except for the town churches in Thayer, Missouri, and Mammoth Spring, Arkansas. My immediate relatives on my mother's side were all members of Churches of Christ. My mother was very active in churches wherever she went.

My father, Benjamin J. Olbricht (1885–1978), stayed in Nebraska when his parents moved to Missouri in 1910. He was sprinkled as an infant in the Catholic Church, but seldom went to Mass in western Nebraska. He bought his parent's land in 1910 and earlier in 1906 homesteaded a section of his own. In the middle 1920s when he met my mother in Missouri he was a rancher with 1440 Nebraska acres. He raised potatoes and took them on the train to Missouri to sell. He started selling potatoes to my grandfather. My grandfather, T. Shelt Taylor, decided that he should introduce his "old maid" school teacher daughter to the Nebraska potato farmer. My parents were married in 1927, when my father was 41 and my mother 29. By 1932 they had four children. I was the second (b. 1929), having an older sister. My sister Nedra's (d. 1988) husband, James R. McGill, is a Church of Christ preacher, as are my two younger brothers Glenn (1931–2012) and Owen (b. 1932).

My mother did not wish to live in western Nebraska, so after a summer there, my parents bought a house in Thayer, Missouri, where I was born. The Church of Christ we first attended was at Centertown, a small community half way between Thayer, Missouri, and Mammoth Spring, Arkansas. My grandfather Taylor was one of the leaders and had given the congregation the land on which the building was constructed. He often taught and preached. That congregation closed when churches were established in Mammoth Spring and Thayer. We first went to Mammoth where my mother was very active. My parents later went to church in Thayer, but I stayed with my grandparents and worked in their gas station, grocery store and attended church with them at Mammoth. Many important Churches of Christ preachers held Gospel meetings in these two congregations, for example, G. K. Wallace, Reuel Lemmons, Cled Wallace, and E. M. Borden, which I attended regularly with my parents. I was baptized in 1946 at age 16 during one of the summer meetings. My religious heritage is therefore deeply Restorationist, more specifically Churches of Christ.[2]

THE ORIGINS OF CHURCHES OF CHRIST IN OREGON COUNTY, MO AND RANDOLPH AND FULTON COUNTY, AR

The roots of Churches of Christ go back to the beginnings of the settlements in these central regions on the Missouri/Arkansas border, possibly as early as 1806.[3] Their evangelistic roots were explicitly those of the second

---

2. Some of this information may be found in my essay, Olbricht, "The Arrival of the Churches of Christ, 74–88. Also some of what is in this chapter may be found in my essay, Olbricht, "Restoration Revivalism," 88–108.

3. Wilson, *Arkansas Christians*, 21.

My Religious Upbringing

Great Awakening. A few early Stoneite settlers arrived on the rivers of Randolph County soon after the Louisiana Purchase in 1803. Most of these people came from Tennessee and Kentucky. Reuel Lemmons, editor of *The Firm Foundation* (1955–1983), whose ancestors came to Randolph County in 1851, claimed that a Christian Church was established at Davidsonville in southwest Randolph County in 1806 by people from Virginia who lived for a time in Tennessee.[4] These early settlers, the Hicks, Cartright, and Pace families were earlier affiliated with the O'Kelly churches in Virginia, then the Stone congregations in Tennessee. From Davidsonville other churches were soon established at Mud Creek in 1815, Fourche De Maux in 1818, and Janes Creek in 1825. About all the names of the people involved were Scotch-Irish except for a few Germans, two of whom were Huffstedler and Von Bauer.[5]

Most of the church plantings of these Restorationists prior to the Civil War were east of Thayer, Missouri, and Mammoth Spring, Arkansas. Sometime after the Civil War Restorationist churches were established in the two towns.[6] Mammoth was probably established even before the Civil War. The church in Thayer was founded after the town was laid out as a rail center in 1882. Max H. Evans, who grew up in Thayer wrote about the founding of the Christian church there.

> My grandfather migrated to Thayer at exactly the same time as Mr. Boughnou's father. . .My grandfather along with his brothers who had already migrated to Oregon County in 1878 and 1880 helped establish a Christian Church which first met at Clifton. The Congregationalist [Church in Thayer] merged into the Christian Church and about 1901 they built the stone building (Christian Church) on Fifth across from the old (1935–1964) High School. . .The first church building in the vicinity was the Clifton School which doubled as a church on weekends with the Baptists, Methodists and Christian groups all using the building which was constructed sometime between 1871 and 1879.[7]

Regarding the background of his grandfather he wrote,

---

4. Lemmons, "A Little Bit of History, 658–661.
5. Morgan, *Arkansas Angels,* vii.
6. Max H. Evans of Houston, Texas, grew up in Thayer. I received this information from him in an e-mail post.
7. Clifton was located north of Warm Fork River toward Alton. In the early days the road followed the Warm Fork and Clifton was about six miles north and west. The region around Clifton had some of the best river bottom farm land in Oregon County.

My ancestors were from Owsley County, Kentucky and Claiborne County, TN before that. They were involved with the Stone-Campbell movement in KY but I have no records. Mr. Boughnou was a Catholic and came from either IL. or Pa. His dad was a locomotive engineer. My grandfather was James A. Evans, Confederate War Veteran, who came to Thayer in 1885. His youngest brother, William Nelson, went to Alton in 1878 as the District Judge then moved to West Plains and eventually became the District Judge there for many years Judge Evans was a mover behind the establishment of Normal Teachers College, now SMU in Springfield.

The churches in Mammoth Spring and Thayer were established before the 1906 Federal Census separation of Christian Churches from Churches of Christ. Likely controversies developed when the two churches commenced using instrumental music, but I never heard anyone set out the specifics. The situation seemed to be live and let live. My grandparents attended the Christian Church in Thayer for a time when they first moved northeast of the town and before they commenced the congregation in their own home in 1921. In our larger family the conclusion was that one should attend a Church of Christ, but if there was none where one lived it was better to go to a Christian church than to none at all. I recall this said of relatives who lived in Humansville, MO and Pocatello, ID. In the 1930s we heard more about controversies with the Christian Churches in Texas and Tennessee from Gospel meeting preachers from those states than from the local leaders of our churches. All of the rural congregations in these three counties were Churches of Christ. Only the churches in Mammoth Spring and Thayer identified themselves as Christian Churches.

The population of Missouri north of the Missouri River was denser than in our region prior to the Civil War. Many of the residents of Northern Missouri had moved from Virginia, Kentucky, or Tennessee. Northeast and central Missouri received the nickname "Little Dixie," because of this migration, and several plantation owners were slave holders.[8] In "Little Dixie" Restorationists, in the 1850s, were the most numerous of all the churches. In 1860 there were about 300 Restorationist congregations and 25,000 members in Missouri. The only states exceeding these numbers were Kentucky, Ohio, Indiana, Tennessee, and Illinois.[9]

The impulse to establish these town congregations may have come from farther north in Missouri, too. There is evidence that Jacob Creath,

---

8. Rafferty, *The Ozarks*, 82.
9. Garrison and DeGroot, *The Disciples of Christ: A History*, 328–329.

My Religious Upbringing

Jr. (1799–1886), a well known Kentucky/Missouri, evangelist visited the region.[10] It may be too that Winthrop H. Hopson (1823–1889) came to these counties in the 1850s. He was born in Kentucky, and his ancestors came from Virginia. He was appointed a state evangelist at Fayette, MO, in 1850.[11]

I have special interest in the Janes Creek congregation because that church was a forerunner of the congregation in which the forebears of T. Shelt Taylor, my mother's father, and his parents were later to be involved. My great-grandparents, John Moody Taylor (1829–1909) and Amy Anthum Waits Taylor (1837–1901) came to Oregon County in 1869 from Franklin County, Alabama. They had thirteen children and by 1919 sixty-eight grandchildren. Most of their descendents into the second generation were members of the Churches of Christ and many into the sixth plus generation.[12] My great-grandfather and his family immediately became involved in the Restorationist churches in the region. In 1877 they moved to Randolph county Arkansas, about twenty miles from their Missouri location. Not only did the Taylors become involved in the churches of the region, their children married spouses who were church members. The congregations include Ring (planted perhaps before the Civil War) and English Bluff (founded in the 1880s?), located along Janes Creek about ten miles south of the Missouri border.[13]

Before my grandfather T. Shelt Taylor died in 1968 my brother Owen Olbricht taped an interview with him regarding his earlier years and transcribed it into a text. Owen asked him about the approach of these churches to evangelism. His depiction sounds much like that of the second Great Awakening. This must have been in the early 1890s.

---

10. Churchill, "Creath, Jacob, Jr.," in Blowers, et al. *The Encyclopedia* 76–77, in a section from Creath's journal Creath mentions being in Oregon County in both 1859 and 1860.

11. "In September, 1850, he was married to Mrs. Ella Lord Chappell, his present wife. The next month, at the State Meeting in Fayette, he was requested to act as Evangelist, and in December he commenced his work. For seven years, he taught a successful female school at Palmyra. He spent the year 1858 traveling in Missouri, Illinois, and Kentucky. Moore, ed., "W. H. Hopson," *Living Pulpit*, Moore, ed. 277–278.

12. This information is taken from genealogical information compiled by Mary Ann Taylor Talley, my third cousin and my mother's brother Wellington Thomas Taylor. Tom, as he was called later in life, was the youngest of the sixty-eight grandchildren.

13. I grew up in Thayer, Missouri, and lived there from 1929–1943. I moved to Alton, Missouri, to live with my Uncle Cleo Taylor in 1943 and stayed until graduating from Alton High in 1947.

Yes. We had a brother in the neighborhood—his name was Uriaus (that is, Daniel Darius) Rose—and he was a wonderful preacher and a good man and they didn't anybody take much interest in church them days and if a man believed and was baptized, people used to laugh and say he's afraid he's going to die and they didn't have sense enough to know everybody had to die it seemed and thought a fellow was a coward that'd be baptized into the church. Brother Rose—the way they had preaching in them days was mostly in the summertime—they didn't preach much in the winter—and my dad used to get them a shoulder of meat or middlin' and give it to Brother Rose and he'd pick out a place somewhere and have him announce that he'd preach there that day and they'd meet and people would get on their horses and ride for twelve, fifteen miles to hear brother Rose preach and I remember one time, he preached for three hours in one sermon and they never quit in less than an hour, hour and a half. But he preached three hours that day and my dad give him a bushel of corn and a middlin' of meat or shoulder of meat and sent him to this place and that place and have it announced a month ahead and he'd go there and preach and once in awhile, they'd have dinner on the ground. He'd preach at eleven o'clock and then again in the afternoon.

Daniel Darius Rose was descended from Daniel Rose (1791–1865) ordained in York, Maine, in 1825. One of the ties of Janes Creek was with Daniel Rose, who was probably born in Pennsylvania or perhaps Maine. His grandfather was born in the Netherlands. In 1825 he was ordained as a Christian (Jones/Smith) preacher in York County, Maine, the county in which I resided from 1997 to 2013. The Jones/Smith people had made considerable headway in Maine and on east into New Brunswick and Nova Scotia. By 1832 Rose commenced a westward migration. His first son John was possibly born in Indiana in 1832. His second son who is more important for our history, Napoleon Bonaparte, "Bone," was born in Missouri, perhaps Oregon County in 1834, and Daniel's later children in either Missouri or Arkansas.[14] In fact the state line was not well defined in that region in the 1830s. Rose probably preached in southern Missouri or Northern Arkansas as early as 1833. In the 1830s he spent much time in Smithville, Arkansas, in Lawrence County below Randolph County. In 1840 Rose was living in Davidson Township, Randolph County, and was accepted as a Christian Church preacher in a conference at the Janes Creek meeting house. From what we can find out, persons from O'Kelly, Jones/Smith,

---

14. Wilson, *Arkansas Christians*, 332.

My Religious Upbringing

Stone, and Campbell backgrounds all joined together in the churches even though they did not do so in their own regions in the east.

Of special interest is that my great-grandfather's oldest son Simion Peter Taylor (1856–1939) married Mary Almanza Rose (1862–1939). Manzy, as she was called, was the granddaughter of Daniel Rose. Her father was Napoleon Bonaparte Rose (1834–1884), who according to family traditions studied law in Chicago. Another son of John Moody, John Calhoun Taylor, (1860–1940) married Harriett James (1865–1940), who was the daughter of Helen Rose James, a daughter of Daniel Rose. A brother of Manzy, that is, a son of Napoleon Boneparte Rose, Daniel Darius Rose (1859–1933), became a Restorationist preacher and preached, probably monthly, as was the custom, in several congregations attended by my great-grandparents and their descendents in Randolph County. These include Ring and English Bluff. By 1900 Daniel Darius Rose lived in various places in Oklahoma and Texas, moving to Brownwood in 1915.

According to a history of the Church of Christ in Thayer, a group of men from Thayer and Mammoth and their families started meeting in the double living room of my grandfather's house half way between Thayer and Mammoth in 1921. These included Benjamin Monroe Lemmons, who was born in Randolph County and moved to Mammoth Spring, Fulton County, Arkansas, in 1905,[15] Lemmons' son-in-law Tom Griffith, my grandfather T. Shelt Taylor, Jim Perrin, and Marshall Holloway. The congregation grew enough by 1925 so that they met in the Ward School. By 1928 they built a building in Centertown, across the highway from my grandfather's gas station and grocery, on land given by my grandfather where some continued to meet until 1936. My earliest memories of church gatherings were at this plain frame building and in the summers at Gospel Meetings outside under the trees between the building and Highway 63, with electric lights strung over head. A Church of Christ congregation was established at Mammoth in 1928 and one at Thayer in 1935. At that time the church at Centertown closed down, and my grandparents and parents participated in the congregation at Mammoth.[16] In 1950 the Church of Christ in Thayer numbered about 150, while that in Mammoth Spring around 200.

---

15. Morgan, *Arkansas Angels*, 50.

16. Don Deffenbaugh, "Reports From the Good Ol' Days." I have a copy probably published in the *Thayer News*.

MISSOURI MEMORIES, 1934–1947

FOUR PROMINENT PREACHERS AT THE END OF THE NINETEENTH CENTURY

The churches in this region were promoted and cared for by permanent residents rather than preachers. Often these men were called elders. They included such persons as Napoleon Bonaparte Rose, J. A. Dubois, "Lum" Kellett, Isaac James, Tom Griffith, Jim Martin, John Moody Taylor, T. Shelt Taylor, Peter Taylor, and Jim Henry Taylor. These "lay leaders," though no distinction was made between clergy and lay leaders in Churches of Christ due to a claim that there were no "clergy" in the New Testament church, sometimes preached, or perhaps more descriptive taught a section of Scripture when the preachers were not available. The preachers lived in the communities where there were churches, but they often preached elsewhere. They held evangelistic meetings, or Gospel Meetings as our people called them, and engaged in religious debates with the Baptists, Methodists, Presbyterians, and Seven Day Adventists. When they did preach at the congregation where they lived, it was normally only once a month. The rest of the time they filled monthly appointments at neighboring congregations. These preachers served under no organization or board and preached whenever and wherever they liked, or were invited. They were paid very little, and most were farmers or else teachers, lawyers, surveyors, and sometimes politicians.

John L. Fry (1863–1939)

A colorful preacher of the late nineteenth century was John L. Fry. I recall hearing my grandfather talk about him, but to my knowledge I never heard him preach.

Fry was born near Ravenden Springs in Randolph County Arkansas, and named John Leondus. His father was Leondus and his mother Jane.[17] In 1913 he lived in Ravenden Springs and later in Walnut Ridge. He was essentially self-educated but had taught math and was an official country surveyor and a real estate lawyer. He taught school until about 1890 when he started preaching in his late thirties. He preached and held meetings all over south-central Missouri and northern Arkansas. He also encouraged younger men to preach by requesting that they accompany him to his various appointments. In later life he lived in Walnut Ridge, Arkansas.

17. Morgan, *Arkansas Angels*, 27.

Fry was a great believer in the special providence of God. Various persons of the time were influenced by the work of George Mueller of Bristol, England, including James A. Harding after whom Harding University is named.[18] Boyd Morgan reported this account of Fry's generosity:

> A great believer in Divine Providence of God I remember him telling of a time when he and his wife moved near a school where he taught and there was no church in the community. They had only twenty dollars, he said. I forget the preacher's name but they arranged for him to come and when the preacher got on his horse to leave Brother Fry gave him the twenty dollars which was every cent they had. "Folks, do you know what happened? The very next day, some men came to get me to survey out a piece of land. Do you know what they paid me? Twenty Dollars." It became a part of his personal proof of bread cast on the waters returning to the giver. He believed in giving and that God would multiply the gift in return to the giver.[19]

Fry was often called when debates were in the making, often in small towns.[20] He was called to Gainesville, Arkansas, in Green County north of Paragould, to debate J. W. Rogers, a general Baptist. Rogers affirmed the first proposition, "The Church of Christ was established in the days of Christ's personal ministry." Fry affirmed the second proposition, "The Church of Christ of which I am a member was established on the first Pentecost after the resurrection." Rogers affirmed the third, "The General Baptist Church of which I am a member, is scriptural in origin, doctrine, name, faith, and practice." Fry affirmed the fourth and last, "The Church of Christ of which I am a member is scriptural in the conditions of pardon and name." T. T. Pack who reported the debate in the *Gospel Advocate* declared that Fry was able to show from all the Scriptures cited by Rogers that the Churches of Christ perspective was the correct one.[21]

Benjamin Monroe Lemmons (1870–1946)

Monroe Lemmons lived in Mammoth Spring, Fulton County, Arkansas, beginning 1905 and preached and held meetings throughout the region. He

---

18. Sears, *The Eyes of Jehovah*.
19. *Ibid.*, 28.
20. On religious debates in America, see: Holifield, *Era of Persuasion*.
21. Published in Morgan, *Arkansas Angels*, 30.

was involved with congregations in which my grandfather T. Shelt Taylor was a leader. I recall hearing him preach in the middle 1930s.[22] He was descended from a family of preachers who were especially noted in Randolph County, the progenitor having moved to Randolph County from Tennessee in 1851. The grandfather of B. M. Lemmons was John M. Lemmons (1816–1898), who was born in Virginia, but moved to Tennessee and was living in Warren County in 1844, where he served as a Baptist minister. They moved to Iowa for a year, but returned to Tennessee. About 1850 they moved to Arkansas. John Lemmons established the Blue Springs church in Independence County, Arkansas; then he and Daniel Rose were selected as evangelists by a district cooperative meeting.[23] Lemmons moved to Hubble Creek in Randolph County and in 1857 built a meeting house. He, Daniel Rose, and others preached for the various churches in that area. During the Civil War the Lemmons favored the Union, which made it difficult in an area where the Confederacy prevailed, so they moved to Johnson County, Illinois.[24] They returned to Randolph County in the summer of 1865.

The father of B. Monroe Lemmons was Amos Josephus (A. J.) Lemmons (1843–1895). Josephus was the son of John Lemmons. Jospehus was born in Tennessee, but grew up in Randolph County. He volunteered for the Union Army and fought at Pea Ridge.[25] Later he moved with his family to Illinois, but returned to Randolph County in 1865. From then on he planted many churches in the region and preached for others until his death.

Benjamin Monroe Lemmons was born in Randolph County. He started preaching in 1895.[26] He moved to Mammoth Spring, Fulton County, Arkansas, in 1905 and established and preached in churches around the region until his death. He was active in the efforts to establish Churches

---

22. Boyd Morgan in *Arkansas Angels* described him, "As a man his life, his habits, his speech was very clean. He opposed sin with all his being and was an extremely great exhorter. A portly man of medium build, he was of open countenance and looked the purity of life which he preached and exemplified. He was one of the most punctual men I have ever known, and it was my conviction that he never was late for anything in his life. He was among the first present for church services and usually a good hour early at the train station when he had to catch a train. (p. 50)

23. Wilson, *Arkansas Christians*, 266.

24. Ibid., 269.

25. Ibid., 271.

26. Morgan, *Arkansas Angels*, 50.

My Religious Upbringing

of Christ in Mammoth Spring and Thayer.[27] Others also involved were my grandfather T. Shelt Taylor, Lemmons' son-in-law, Tom Griffith, Jim Perrin, and Marshall Holloway.

Monroe Lemmons preached at these congregations when requested and traveled throughout the region to hold meetings and encourage the churches. In those days plain and argumentative preaching sometimes elicited violent reactions. Boyd Morgan tells of the following threat to Lemmons:

> Such a warning came to him from a woman on one of his appointments at Bald Knob (near Mammoth Spring, Arkansas). He was told that if he came back to his next appointment there, that she would be where he crossed the creek with a shotgun and he would never get across. He thought it rather amusing, but his family did not. When the Lord's Day for the appointment came, he saddled his horse and started for Bald Knob. He reassured his family saying: "I am not one bit afraid I can't cross the creek." Sure enough on the creek sat the woman with her shotgun on her lap. Brother Lemmons never hesitated or stopped at all. He just rode on across the creek. Not a word was said or a shot fired. He preached as usual.[28]

Preachers in those days had to be courageous, committed and frugal.

Bynum Black (1871–1944)

Bynum Black was born in Ravenden Springs, Sharp County, Arkansas, to Elic and Harriet Black. His father and two brothers left Ireland because of the potato famine in Ireland 1845–1851, and first moved to Missouri, then to Sharp County.[29] The father was a school teacher. Black married Maggie English of Randolph County in 1890. Her brother Will English was married to Nancy Taylor English, a niece of my grandfather, T. Shelt Taylor. Almost immediately Black started making talks in church and baptized a man the next Sunday. In 1896 Bynum Black baptized my recently-married grandparents, T. Shelt and Myrtle Dunsmore Taylor, in Janes Creek in Randolph County. Black moved to Oklahoma from Randolph County in 1914

---

27. *Ibid.*, 275.
28. Morgan, *Arkansas Angels*, 51.
29. Smith, "Bynum Black," *Gospel Preachers of Yesteryear* 38–51.

and spent the rest of his life there. Nevertheless, he was influential in our region in the twenty-some years he preached there.

Black farmed as well as preached. He also held meetings in the region and helped W. F. Lemmons, a grandson of John M. Lemmons, produce a religious paper *Eye Openers*, published in Ravenden Springs. Like Fry, more than once Black was threatened. Black preached the strict statements of Jesus about divorce, and one woman, convinced by his declarations, decided to leave her husband, because he had been divorced. The husband in turn threatened to kill Black. Black took the threat seriously, and members of the congregation took a knife away from the husband who declared that he would cut Black's throat.[30] Black also held several debates with a well-known Arkansas Missionary Baptist Minister, Ben M. Bogard.[31] He also debated several Mormons. Regarding his debating Boyd Morgan wrote,

> A very noble debater, his services were solicited far and wide to defend the gospel. I feel certain, but for Bynum Black that Northeast Arkansas would have several Mormon churches today. He ably routed them from the polemic platform until they just disappeared. Once at Williford [Sharp County] Arkansas, he debated a Mormon named Ward. This debate was scheduled for nine days. Mr. Ward said that if Bro. Black would prove what he said about Joseph Smith that he (Ward) would quit debating. Bro. Black proved it, and Mr. Ward proved a man of his word. He not only quit debating and quit preaching and went into the mercantile business.[32]

Joe H. Blue (1875–1954)

Joe Blue was born near Mt. Pleasant in Izard County, Arkansas, Southwest of Salem. His family moved to Independence County, then when Joe was 11 to Fulton County near Salem. His father was a Church of Christ preacher, and Joe was one of twelve children. He was baptized at 16. He struggled to attend school. When he was 17 he traded a mule for a year of education, a deal opposed by his father. He traveled with preachers who held meetings and started preaching near Poughkeepsie in Sharp County in 1896. He wrote concerning these beginnings,

30. Morgan, *Arkansas Angels*, 54.
31. Foreman and Payne, *The Life and Works of Benjamin Marcus Bogard*.
32. Morgan, *Arkansas Angels*, 54.

My Religious Upbringing

On November 1, 1896, I preached my first sermon at Lebanon Schoolhouse near Poughkeepsie. I traveled with Brothers George and Garner until Christmas that year, and in that time I preached six times. I then started out by myself. I went into Sharp County and preached out in the sticks, in homes and schoolhouses. I had in my saddle-pockets the same change of clothes, my Bible, the Gospel Plan of Salvation by T. W. Brents[33], and four cents in my pocket. I did not say a word to anyone about my poverty. I was afraid they would think I was preaching for money. I preached all that year (1897) and baptized 75 and established one congregation. The brethren paid me $19.00 for my work that year. In May of that year my father sent me $10.00 to buy me a suit of clothes. I bought them with the $10.00, and then I was in fine shape for the work. Many days I went without dinner because I did not have the money to buy it.[34]

In the fall of 1897 Blue married Mary Montgomery of Morriston, Fulton County, Arkansas. She lived south of Salem not too far from the retirement community, Horseshoe Bend. She owned some livestock. They bought a farm nearby and lived there the rest of their lives. Mary looked after the farm while Joe Blue traversed the region and even into other states proclaiming the word. They were frugal and grew about everything they needed.[35]

Blue was able to win most of his friends and neighbors in the small Morriston community. Before too many years the Baptist, Methodist, Holiness, and Presbyterian churches closed down.[36] Blue supported larger efforts outside the region. He was on the board of Southern Christian Home in Morrilton, Arkansas, and Harding College (now University) at Searcy. I heard Joe Blue preach several times in the last half of the 1930s and early 1940s. For a while in the 1940s he preached once a month at Thayer. But

---

33. Brents, *The Gospel Plan of Salvation*. This was purchased by most Churches of Christ ministers at that time and carried with the Bible.

34. Quoted in Morgan, *Arkansas Angels*, 80.

35. Boyd Morgan wrote about Joe Blue, "Joe H. Blue was a large man, not fat, not slim, just a big man. He stood well above six feet in height and I would guess his weight at 220 pounds. His presence denoted solidarity. He spoke without the slightest doubt of what he said. He preached the Bible. He loved the Bible. He knew the Bible. Above all he believed every word of it. I know that he did. When he spoke, the hearer had the impression that he knew all he needed to know to speak with authority on the subject. Few men could say a thing with equal force to Joe H. Blue." 89.

36. *Ibid.*

this did not last. Some felt his preaching was too abrasive. His voice was gruff, he was didactic and plain spoken. He was past his prime in his late sixties. The last time I saw Joe Blue was in 1948. I was a student at Harding College, Searcy. I boarded the train at Mammoth Spring to ride the Frisco to Hoxie then transfer to the Missouri Pacific to continue to Kensett. When we stopped at Hardy, Arkansas, Joe Blue got on the train along with some other man. I introduced myself. He knew my family well. He started telling stories and entertained us as he so often did all the way to Hoxie.

CONCLUSIONS

In taking up specific persons I conclude that at least ninety percent of the persons who were Restorationists in these three counties were of Scotch-Irish stock. Most of the early Restorationist leaders had migrated more immediately from Kentucky and Tennessee. Others came from Alabama, Virginia, and New England. The second generation soon intermarried so that family networks prevailed in all the churches. What I think is especially noteworthy is that these immigrants came from five different streams of Restorations, and who, though somewhat similar in the regions of their strengths, that is Virginia, New England, Ohio, Virginia, and Kentucky, often worshiped in disparate churches with people from their own regional backgrounds. When these migrants came to Oregon, Randolph, and Fulton Countries, however, as far as we can tell, they all cast their lot with those who arrived first and did not establish churches from their specific backgrounds. From Randolph Country on east to the Mississippi River, in many decades since 1810, people from the Restorationist churches were in the majority as well as in the countryside around Thayer, Missouri, and Mammoth Spring, Arkansas.[37]

---

37. The data may be found in Halvorson and Newman, *Atlas of Religious Change in America.* 179–181.

Chapter VII

Missouri Evangelism

Most of the religionists who settled in central Southern Missouri and Northern Arkansas were heirs of the Reformed (Calvin and Zwingli) Branch of the Protestant Reformation, and of the awakening traditions in American religious history.[1] Revivalism broke out in the Northeast in the 1740s and was modified to comply with the frontier conditions from New Jersey to Massachusetts, then farther south in the first Great Awakening. The second Great Awakening flamed after the Revolutionary War in the early 1800s beginning in Kentucky and Tennessee. The second awakening focused upon extended regional mass gatherings called camp meetings. When Presbyterians, Baptists, Disciples (the Christian Church), and Methodists (and later Pentecostals who emerged from Methodism) moved to Oregon Country, Missouri, and Randolph and Fulton County, Arkansas, they brought their approaches to revivalism with them, modified in various ways to conform with their theology and the circumstances in which they lived.[2]

    1. "The first immigrants were southerners, mainly of Scotch-Irish descent and of the yeoman farmer type, mainly poor, nonslaveholders. Most were from Tennessee, North Carolina, Virginia, Pennsylvania, and Kentucky. Most probably were of the restless frontier type cut in the mold of Daniel Boone and Kit Carson." Rafferty, *The Ozarks: Land and Life,* 46. I am indebted to Brooks Blevins and John Smalzbauer who read an earlier version this essay. I have incorporated their recommendations both interpretive and bibliographical.

    2. "The largest number of early American settlers in the Ozarks were Scotch-Irish. Originally Presbyterian, many had by then moved into Baptist, Methodist or Campbellite

I now will sketch the modifications and changes in the American revivalistic trajectories and show especially the manner in which they influenced the Gospel Meetings of Churches of Christ in Oregon County, MO, and Randolph and Fulton County, AR early in the twentieth century. The religious approach in the Churches of Christ was more didactic and rationalistic, which in turn influenced significantly their adaptation of revivalistic methodologies. I will first set out a brief sketch of awakening evangelism in America, then identify the ties of Churches of Christ in these central counties on the Missouri/Arkansas border with awakening evangelism and finally provide concrete depictions of gospel meetings at the Church of Christ in Mammoth Spring 1930-50.

METHODS IN AMERICAN REVIVALISM

Awakening revivalism has a long history in North America. Scholars who have focused on Protestant revivalism have noted four main surges: (1) The first Great Awakening (1720–1750), (2) The second Areat Awakening (1800–1840), (3) the urban center or prayer meeting revival (1857–1890) and (4) the awakening heralded by the Billy Graham crusades (1949–1960).[3] Each of these epochs had their distinctive modus operandi. Some of these methods have persisted until the present.

It is now commonly agreed that the first Great Awakening had two roots. The first was in the pietistic churches of the Raritan Valley of New Jersey, sparked by the preaching of Theodore Freylinghausen (1691–1747), a Dutch Pietist minister, who arrived in America in 1720.[4] The New Jersey revivals were mostly held in church and/or community buildings, but many times in private dwellings for one or two successive nights. Members from various church groups attended, but persons involved were mostly pietistic Lutherans and Presbyterians. In 1743 the Awakening broke out at Northampton, Massachusetts, where Jonathan Edwards (1703-1758) of

---

persuasions, which seemed better adapted to frontier and post-frontier situations." Burgess, "Perspectives on the sacred: Religion in the Ozarks," 5.

3. Travis, "Protestant Revivalism," *Dictionary of Christianity in America*, 1012–15; McLoughlin, Jr., *Modern Revivalism;*. M Clymond, *Encyclopedia of Religious Revivals in America*; Blumhoffer and Balmer, *Modern Christian Revivals*; Boles, *The Great Revival*; Conkin, *Cane Ridge*.

4. The Pietist movement began in the German Evangelical (Lutheran) Church. The significant early leaders were Philip Jacob Spener (1635–1703) and August Hermann Francke (1663–1727). Pietists spread out of Germany into Holland and elsewhere.

later international acclaim was the minister, fueled by news of happenings in New Jersey and Scotland.[5] Edwards first noticed a growing seriousness in the young people of the congregation. According to Edwards in a letter to Thomas Prince of Boston the revival atmosphere accelerated among these Congregationalists when George Whitefield (1715–1770) the British Methodist evangelist arrived. From these beginnings revival preachers crisscrossed New England and eventually down the coast to Georgia preaching a night or two then moving on.[6]

The second source especially impacted those with Scottish backgrounds, that is the Presbyterians patterned after the Sacramental revivals that commenced in Scotland in the 1740s. Holy fairs often accompanied sacramental (that is, the celebration of the Lord's Supper) observances in Scotland, and in the 1740s became occasions for the outburst of revivals.[7] The greatest of these occurred at Cambuslang in 1742.[8] Since the Holy Fairs were in the open air and since on this occasion more than 30,000 persons were attracted, tents were erected in the church yard and in surrounding fields. Persons came from as far away as Glasgow, Edinburgh, and smaller cities.

The Second Great Awakening broke out in Kentucky early in the nineteenth century chiefly among the Presbyterians and in conjunction with sacramental services. The chief instigator was James McGready (1758–1817) a Presbyterian. McGready first preached in North Carolina, but by 1800 had relocated to Logan County, Kentucky. In July of 1800 in the manner of the Scottish revivals he announced a sacramental service at the Gasper River Presbyterian Church.[9] Hundreds of people heard the announcement and traveled to the site prepared to stay. In these settings the protracted revivals were designated camp meetings.[10] Presbyterians and Methodists did the preaching, and their people attended the meetings. The Baptists conducted their revivals independently and not connected with sacramental services.

---

5. Sometimes designated the foremost original American theologian, Edwards was educated at Yale and at his death was president of Princeton.

6. Gaustad, *The Great Awakening*. On Whitefield in America see: http://www.nhinet.org/ccs/docs/awaken.htm.

7 Schmidt, *Holy Fair*.

8. Macfarlan, *The revivals of the Eighteenth Century*.

9 B. L. Shelly, "James McGready," *Dictionary of Christianity in America*. 687f.

10 Johnson, *The Frontier Camp Meeting*; Bruce, Jr., *And They All Sang Hallelujah*; Eslinger, *Citizens: The Social Origins*.

The most famous of all the early camp meetings was launched at Cane Ridge northeast of Lexington, Kentucky, in August of 1801. The person who conceived and orchestrated the meeting was Barton Warren Stone (1772-1844), minister for the Presbyterian churches at Cane Ridge and Concord. He was joined by several Presbyterian, a few Methodists preachers, and one Baptist.[11] He was the Stone after whom the Stone-Campbell movement of which Churches of Christ are a part was named. The crowds gathered in wagons starting on Friday Night and grew to be as many as perhaps 25,000 persons. Four or five preaching stands were erected throughout the area, and preachers speaking simultaneously in different areas regaled the crowds as they gathered round.[12] The Cane Ridge camp meeting continued on location for six or seven days, whereupon the attendees packed up their wagons in order to return home.

What was surprising was the exercises involved especially the falling which had occurred neither in Scotland nor the Northeast. Several years later Barton W. Stone published an *Autobiography* in which he described in some detail the proceedings.

> The bodily agitations or exercises, attending the excitement in the beginning of this century, were various, and called by various names;—as, the falling exercise—the jerks—the dancing exercise—the barking exercise—the laughing and singing exercise, &c.—The falling exercise was very common among all classes, the saints and sinners of every age and of every grace, from the philosopher to the clown. The subject of this exercise would, generally, with a piercing scream, fall like a log on the floor, earth, or mud, and appear as dead.[13]

The camp meetings were new American Second Awakening phenomena. People arrived in wagons from greater distances and camped on the grounds.

Revivals took a somewhat different form under Charles Finney (1792-1875), the first American to organize large assemblies in cities. Finney became a Presbyterian revivalist in upstate New York doing one night stands in several places in Oneida County. In the years 1827-1832 Finney evangelized in New York City, Philadelphia, Boston, and Rochester,

---

11 Eslinger, 208.

12. Stone, *A Short History*. 67.

13 *Ibid.*, 69.

launching meetings several nights in a row.[14] The short gatherings of the earlier years of the Second Awakenings now turned into lengthy efforts sometimes designated protracted meetings.

The major launching of extended revivals was the contribution of Dwight L. Moody (1837–1899) a few years after the prayer meeting awakening that began in 1857.[15] Moody was from a Congregational and Presbyterian background, but became Independent. The first major successes of Moody were in Great Britain, where from 1873–1875 he held nightly preaching sessions in England, Scotland, and Ireland. His acclaim in Great Britain now commended Moody to American audiences and he launched protracted engagements in Brooklyn, New York City, Chicago, and Boston. The nightly gatherings in New York lasted for four months in 1876.[16]

In the 1930s revivals were standard annual or more affairs in many American Protestant Churches. Because of the successes of Finney and Moody revivals continued for several days and were prepared for and announced weeks in advance. In the early twentieth century the revivals and the evangelists tended to function within the parameters of denominational boundaries. Their *modus operandi* therefore reflected the theology and outlook of the various confessional groups. Standard revivals lasted a week or more. In the cities and towns they were held in churches or large auditoriums but also in tents on vacant lots. Throughout the countryside evangelists utilized tents, brush arbors, and groves. Most churches in the Ozarks, including Churches of Christ, conducted revivals that drew upon two hundred years of America awakening procedures.

GOSPEL MEETINGS OF THE 1930S AND 1940S

The main avenue for the steady stream of ingathering in the central Ozark Churches of Christ was the gospel meeting. Patterned in a modified form of the awakening revivals and the later protracted meetings, these efforts were distinguished by reasoned teaching rather than excessive emotionalism. It's not that Churches of Christ gospel meeting were without emotions, but they were expressed in a different way. That is why Churches of Christ leaders preferred the terminology "gospel meeting" to "revival," the standard

---

14. Hambrick-Stowe, *Charles G. Finney.*
15 Olbricht, "Prayer Meeting," *Dictionary of Christianity in America,* 922.
16 Weisberger, *They Gathered at the River,* 205.

awakening nomenclature. They wished to downplay the vocal and bodily aspects of revivals and highlight preaching the New Testament.

The common conviction of evangelists from Reformed (Calvinistic) backgrounds, as were most of those in the two /great Awakenings, was that salvation came about through the work of the Holy Spirit upon the unconverted. The purpose of revivals was therefore to warn people of their unsaved state and stress the need for repentance. It was incumbent upon unbelievers to seek an overpowering event which was to be identified as the indwelling of the Holy Spirit. In other words on this momentous occasion the unbeliever experienced a Holy Spirit conversion initiated by God himself. This experiential conversion became the grounds for the assurance of salvation and the declaration of the experience the basis for church membership. In the Second Awakening those involved in this emotional search were invited into a place for special struggling—the enclosed pen in the camp meetings or the mourner's bench in the churches.[17]

Both Alexander Campbell and Walter Scott of the Stone-Campbell movement in the first half of the nineteenth century rejected the standard Calvinistic view of conversion even though they grew up in Presbyterian congregations. They concluded that conversion came about through hearing the story (the gospel) of Christ preached. God and his Son provided the good news that as the result of Jesus' death all those who heard, believed, and were baptized into Jesus Christ had their sins washed away. These actions of God and their acceptance became the grounds of their salvation. It was only then that the Holy Spirit entered into their lives.[18] Scott made the contrast between his former Calvinist views and the one he believed affirmed in Scriptures.

> Is it by special and distinct operations upon the mind of the sinner before faith, as all your systems of divinity assert? or does he, for the purpose of producing faith and life in us, adduce testimony—divine testimony of the holy scripture? We Reformers [the Stone-Campbell Christians] assert the latter, as the true state of the case, and it is a proposition which derives proof and illustration from every individual conversion noticed in scripture; a proposition in harmony, as well with fact and scripture, as with reason and the

---

17. For the initiating in the second awakening of the invitation to the pen or mourner's bench for the conversion struggle see Olbricht "The Invitation—A Survey," 6–16. http://www.acu.edu/sponsored/restoration_quarterly/archives/1960s/vol_5_no_1_contents/olbricht.html.

18 Olbricht, "The Holy Spirit in the Early Restoration Movement."

common experience of mankind. Is it in the annals of humanity, that men, endowed with the reasonability common to their species, ever obtained faith in anything earthly or divine, but by means of testimony?[19]

Walter Scott changed the goal of preaching among those in the Stone-Campbell movement. Rather than the traditional inviting sinners to struggle for conversion in the pen or on the mourner's bench, he invited them to hear the preaching of the gospel then respond by coming forward in order to request baptism by immersion. In his book, *The Gospel Restored*, he reported at some length on the reasons for this changed view and the practical enactment of it in 1827 in his evangelizing on the Western Reserve.[20] The ancient gospel, as Scott presented it, consisted of human action in hearing, believing, and being baptized and God's response through forgiveness of sin, the gift of the Holy Spirit, and eternal salvation.[21]

I myself experienced the emotive difference in attending revivals at Pentecostal and Baptist revivals. In the late 1930s my mother and I visited a revival going on at the Greentown Assembly of God. This church, just south of the Thayer city limits and west of highway 63, was comprised of many of the descendents of my grandmother Taylor's sister, Mattie Dunsmore Green. Most of the preaching consisted of emotionally-laden phrases in rising and lowering volume. People fell in the aisles and were covered with a black cloth. In the nineteen forties I attended a Baptist revival with my Uncle Cleo near Hickory Grove northeast of Alton. While the preacher had an outlined message he spoke as loud as he could, often gasping for air. His speech cadences were sing-song and emotive. In contrast the speaking in Churches of Christ gospel meetings was didactic, the preacher often employing chart outlines imprinted on oil cloth which could be rolled up and used elsewhere or written on a blackboard.[22]

Every preacher in Churches of Christ during the decades of the 30s and 40s held gospel meetings, even if spending the winter months in one locality. He spent spring, summer, and fall months conducting gospel meetings wherever invited. The meetings were held in groves, under tents or

---

19. Scott, *The Evangelist*, (1832) 27.

20. Scott, *The Gospel Restored*.

21. Hughes, *Reviving the Ancient Faith,* 48–54. For places in which gospel meetings are discussed.

22. For descriptions of the evangelism of various denominations: Hill, *One Name but Several Faces;* Leonard, *Christianity in Appalachia;* Gilmore, Ozark Baptizings.

brush arbors, on vacant lots, and in public buildings. Most new Churches of Christ were planted by first holding a gospel meeting. These efforts were highly successful because there were few public gatherings in most of the communities. Churches of Christ preachers who became known through conducting meetings included T. B. Larimore, David Lipscomb, James A. Harding, T. W. Brents, R. L. Whiteside, C. R. Nichol, N. B. Hardeman, G. C. Brewer, Marshall Keeble, and Foy E. Wallace, Jr. Even well-educated preachers, including Hall Calhoun (1863–1935), with a Ph.D. in Old Testament from Harvard Divinity School and L. C. Sears (1895–1985), Dean of Harding College with a Ph.D. in English from the University of Chicago, delighted in holding gospel meetings. While gospel meetings still persist in some Churches of Christ and in rural areas they are much less successful because of competition—first with movies, then television, and also organized public school and professional sports activities.

Gospel meetings in Churches of Christ varied in length in the early part of the twentieth century, but by the 1930s tended to last two weeks through three Sundays. Night meetings were well attended by church members, their friends, neighbors, and relatives, and drop-ins. Held under tents, these meetings employed public address systems, and people often sat in cars and listened. Sometimes in small towns the people present at the final night sessions of the meetings might total more than the town population because of those who drove in from the countryside and neighboring towns.

The Churches of Christ in Mammoth Spring, Arkansas, and Thayer, Missouri, where I attended through the forties until I went to Harding College in 1947, held gospel meetings each summer in late July or early August. The weather was normally pleasant at night with few rains. Since many people came from farms, the singing and preaching did not commence until 8:00 P. M. so that the farmers were out of the fields and those with dairy cattle through milking. The church in Mammoth in the summers of 1937 to 1939 employed G. K. Wallace of Wichita, Kansas, as the evangelist. Wallace was from a large group of about a dozen related Churches of Christ preachers. Foy E. Wallace, Jr., and Glenn Wallace were two of the best known. The people of our region knew of the Wallaces because Glenn Wallace preached in Springfield, Missouri, from 1931–1937 and spoke daily on a radio station to which we listened. The first summer G. K. Wallace held a meeting in Mammoth the congregation had recently completed a native stone building that would seat about 180. The attendance in the winter was normally somewhat above a hundred. G. K. Wallace used to visit Abilene Christian when I taught there from 1967–1986 to see his daughter and son-in-law Ben Zickefoose who was a physical education instructor. Wallace remembered my family and occasionally talked with me about Mammoth. He baptized my father. He told me that he baptized a total of 105 persons in those three summer meetings. That is not a large number, but the town of Mammoth had a population of less than five hundred. The result was that the congregation almost doubled in size in those three years.

Revivals in the region tended to be out of doors, but were sometimes in buildings. Various places were identified as suitable: groves, campgrounds, or brush arbors along roadsides. Brush arbors were constructed on upright poles upon which pole "rafters" were laid horizontally. Leafed branches were placed on top of the rafters to ward off the sun and/or light rain. The preferred place for the gospel meeting at both Thayer and Mammoth was a large tent located on the church lot at the side or back of the building. Our churches by that time had become too sophisticated for brush arbors.

Various means were employed to announce the Gospel Meetings. A favorite manner was the printing of posters about fifteen by thirty inches to be placed in store windows in Thayer and Mammoth. The poster included a picture of the evangelist and details regarding dates, times, and topics. Announcements were sent to and broadcasted on Churches of Christ radio programs in West Plains, Springfield, and Poplar Bluff. Ads were placed in the *Thayer News* and the *Democrat* of Mammoth Spring. People were encouraged to invite relatives, friends and neighbors. At times public address systems for cars were rented, and someone drove up and down the streets and country lanes announcing the meetings as happened when the circus came to town.

The large rented tent with folding chairs seated about 300. Chairs were also placed on the periphery. Though tents came with sides these were normally kept rolled up unless a blowing rain passed through. At the back of the tent a platform about two feet high and ten by twelve feet was constructed. On the rear of the platform a large blackboard was attached on a frame. The song leader directed from the platform, and the preacher spoke from a small stand in the middle. A public address system was not employed in the church buildings at either Thayer or Mammoth so the church rented one for the meeting. Often those who wanted to hear the preaching but did not wish to mingle with the people parked on the streets near the tent, rolled down the widows, and listened as they sat in their car. It was estimated that

Saturday and Sunday nights at Mammoth Spring 500 to 600 persons could be found in and around the tent. People from Thayer attended the meetings as well as those from the countryside. The population of Mammoth then was somewhat more than 500.

The topics upon which Wallace spoke in each of those Mammoth meetings were fairly typical. He commenced with a focus on the church: its name—that is, Church of Christ—its identity—that is, its congregational status—its officers, and its worship. Often too, sermons were preached on undenominational Christianity and the "Restoration Plea." Wallace declared that his brethren were Christians only and encouraged unity, liberty for divine authority over human, loyalty to Christ rather than to a party, and advancement in the discovery and practice of the divine truth. In the second week sermons shifted to a focus on the gospel plan of salvation—usually one night each on hearing, believing, repenting, confessing, and being baptized. The final sermons detailed the contrasting joys of heaven and tortures of hell. I still recall Wallace writing, in regard to a sermon on salvation 1. Hear, 2. Believe, 3. Repent, 4. Confess, 5. Be baptized, along with the chapter and verses of appropriate scriptures, on the blackboard, a line for each of the five.

Each session began with rousing singing, a prayer, and then the sermon which tended to be an hour or longer. Toward the conclusion Wallace exhorted the people either to be baptized or to commit themselves to faithful church involvement anew ("being restored"). The song leader then sprang up, signaled for the crowd to arise, and launched into the invitation song. The exhortations became importunate more than the body of the sermon, encouraging "sinners" to consider the shortness of life, the desire of their friends and loved ones for them to be baptized, and the allures of heaven. As long as people responded, verses of a song, for example, "Just As I Am" continued after a new exhortation. Baptisms were administered nightly. Several in the Mammoth congregation drove around the spring to the location at which the Warm Fork entered into Spring River below the dam. A few of the cars directed their headlights toward the river. The preacher and those to be baptized waded out. After the baptisms the crowd burst into song, "O happy day, when Jesus washed my sins away." People embraced the baptized and all went home rejoicing in their newly found or strengthened faith. These were emotional times with not a few tears flowing, especially by those who had waited a long time for their loved ones to obey the gospel.

Often morning sessions were held Monday through Saturday in the church building, mostly attended by members. The morning sermons centered on diligent involvement in church activities and a deepening of a personal spiritual life.

The Churches of Christ gospel meetings of that era were highly successful in raising the level of awareness of spirituality in the churches and the communities in which they were held. These were special times for spiritual formation of youth, encouragement to active church involvement and leadership among the adults, and decisions to preach the gospel among young men.

In the 1930s when Wallace preached in the meetings at Mammoth a congregational picnic was held in the park on the last Sunday after the morning service. Members brought prepared food, normally fried chicken, potato salad, and green beans and for desert lemon, chocolate, and apple pies. After the lunch, a song director led a few songs. Preachers were encouraged to entertain in some manner, and each had a specialty. The summers G. K. Wallace held the meetings the attendees were alerted as someone backed up a flat bed truck. Wallace climbed up, tucked his tie in his shirt, rolled up his sleeves then proceeded to walk on his hands around the truck bed with his legs drooping at the knees. Other evangelists rendered declamations.

Churches of Christ preachers who held Gospel Meetings in Oregon County, Missouri, and Fulton County, Arkansas, were heirs of two centuries of awakening revivalism in America. They modified these occasions so as to conform to their theology and purposes. Rather than invite sinners to "pray through" on mourner's benches, they invited those influenced by the preaching to obey "from the heart that form of doctrine" by being baptized. The preaching tended to emphasize head knowledge rather than what was felt in the heart. In the 1930s Churches of Christ gospel meetings had become standardized and normally were held once a year in July and August for two weeks, beginning and ending on Sunday. These were intensive spiritually uplifting days on which those who had not yet committed their lives to Jesus Christ were baptized in his name and added to his church. Members were re-encouraged and confirmed to a higher level of dedication.

Chapter VIII

―――

War

"Life did not stop, and one had to live."
Leo Tolstoy, *War and Peace*

The morning of December 7, 1941, dawned gray and cool. Following our usual routine we prepared to go to Bible Study and worship at the Mammoth Spring Church of Christ. Our extended family included my grandparents, T. Shelt and Myrtle Taylor, my parents, Ben and Agnes Olbricht, and my three siblings, Nedra, Glenn and Owen, my Uncle and Aunt Cleo and Ova Taylor and their young daughter Barbara Ann, and a nephew of both my grandparents, Bynum Dunsmore, his wife Opal, and their son James Ray. After church was over we gathered at my grandparents as we normally did for Sunday dinner. The adults always ate first, then the children. We kids didn't worry since there was always food enough. We stayed outside and tossed around a football or softball. After all of us had eaten, Uncle Cleo and five of the kids, my sister included, climbed the stile over the back fence into grandpa's cow pasture and played football.

Football was our favorite game in the fall. The air that day was crisp, but we kept warm through vigorous play. We had been back and forth across the pasture about an hour when Bynum came out the back door of the house, down the steps and over the stile. He shouted and finally got our attention. He yelled, "The Japs bombed Pearl Harbor." At first his report didn't fully register, so we kept playing. But finally we decided to head to the house and listen to my grandfather's Philco radio. The news came fast and furious. The bombing created great panic and havoc at this idyllic yet crucial naval base.

I turned twelve the month before. Now the halcyon days of youth faded into oblivion. I quickly came of age. In another two years I entered Alton, Missouri, high school in the fall of 1943. The war raged on. The news of lost battles constantly bombarded the radio waves and the newsreels at our movie theatre. The invasion of Normandy Beach was still a year away. In the next two years I learned with growing skill to navigate the far-reaching impact of war and in my final year of high school, an astounding peace. These years remain indelibly etched in my thoughts—momentous Missouri memories. These long months comprised my own boot camp, not for military service, but for the battle of life.

ALTON HIGH SCHOOL

My first eight years of schooling occurred at Thayer Elementary, a two story brick building on Sixth Street high above the downtown business district. We lived a half mile from the school, just south of the Thayer city limit. Through a somewhat unusual set of circumstances my high school years occurred at Alton High School seventeen miles to the northeast, the county seat of Oregon County, Missouri. My grandfather, Henry Olbricht, born in Glatz, Silesian Province, Germany, homesteaded in Sioux County, Nebraska, in 1892. He first homesteaded 160 acres then when the Kinkaid Homesteading Act (1904) passed for western Nebraska, he filed a claim on a section, that is, 640 acres. When my father, Benjamin J. Olbricht (1885–1978) reached 21 he filed on a contiguous section. In 1911 my German grandparents sold their Nebraska land consisting of 800 acres to my father and moved to a farm on the upper reaches of Janes Creek east of Thayer, Missouri. My father lived and worked the Nebraska ranch of 1440 acres until he and my mother—born in Arkansas, but grew up in Missouri, east of Thayer—were married in 1927.

From my early years I heard my father speak glowingly of the ranch. Had it been just him he would have continued living in Nebraska. Some of the drama of my young years was when about every five years my father went down to the Thayer depot and boarded a train for Crawford, Nebraska, a thousand miles northwest. Otherwise he seldom traveled beyond

Oregon County and Fulton County in Arkansas. The Nebraska trip was a major undertaking for him and surreal for me, this young lad of six.

We did a bit of farming on our Missouri eleven acres and raised chickens and milk cows. My grandfather nearby grew alfalfa and atlas sargo and kept beef cattle on 40 acres. I enjoyed farm activities. I therefore dreamed of the west glamorized by Gene Autry and Roy Rogers movies and the exploits of Theodore Roosevelt. I had a guaranteed easy foot in the door of ranching, far more land in the Nebraska ranch than held by most of my Missouri farming relatives. My father encouraged my dream of taking over his ranch.

My family believed in preparation for a life's work. Not only did one need experience, of which I could get plenty in Missouri, but education. My Uncle Cleo Taylor was the vocational agriculture teacher at Alton High School. The teaching of agriculture in high schools, supported by federal funding, commenced in 1917 with the Smith-Hughes Act. It was decided by my family and my Uncle that I should live with him in Alton, work on his ranch of above a thousand acres, and attend Alton High School. I could take courses in agriculture all four years. At that time Thayer did not have a vocational agricultural program. Upon graduating from high school I would then proceed to the University of Missouri and take a degree in agriculture. With all that experience and education I should be adequately prepared to successfully operate our heritage Nebraska ranch. Declaration of war changed various aspects of farming and high school education 1943-1947, but it was a time when life focused more sharply on the task at hand— at least the life that unfolded before me.

MILITARY SERVICE

The reality of the war set in when civilian relatives were inducted and scattered throughout the world in various wartime operations. First to go were two of my cousins, Elmer and Albert Prewitt. Both of these men as high school students lived with my grandfather, T. Shelt Taylor, and graduated from Thayer High. Their parents lived twenty miles southeast of Thayer beyond Wirth, Arkansas, in a sparsely settled region. Completing high school for them was difficult at best, so they stayed with my grandfather and grandmother and worked at his gas station/small grocery. They were inducted within the first year of the war. Elmer and Albert had become close companions to my brothers and me. I knew Albert best. He was a flight engineer aboard a B-24 bomber and a decorated World War II veteran with many medals, including one with three bronze stars and another with three flying oak clusters and the distinguished flying crosses. Elmer and Albert had a younger brother Perry Prewitt who was not so fortunate. Perry spent part of his high school years with Uncle Cleo and Aunt Ova and graduated from Alton High in 1942. He was soon thereafter inducted into the army and served through the war, but was killed April 25, 1945 in Europe in an accident in which he was unloading munitions from a truck shortly after the war with Germany ended.

My mother's brother, Norval Taylor, was inducted next and toward war's end my mother's youngest brother Wellington (Tom) Taylor. The remaining brother of my mother, Cleo Taylor, was not drafted because he was a vocational agriculture teacher and operated a fairly large farm. Uncle Norval left Thayer 3:00 A. M. on the morning of December 15, 1942, to be inducted into the army at Jefferson Barracks, Missouri, just south of St. Louis. His departure was especially painful to my grandmother, but also to granddad. No one in the immediate family had served in the military since the Civil War. A number of Church of Christ preachers and members questioned Christians killing others even in war, and some of them were conscientious objectors. My grandparents did not go to that extreme, but they disavowed a warring spirit and opposed the United States entering military operations on foreign soil.

I slept at that time in my grandparents' second floor dormered bedroom. About 2:30 A.M. on the 15th I was awakened by my grandmother. I knew my Uncle was leaving but I had already said goodbye the night before. My grandmother started talking quietly. She said, "Your mother gave you a small New Testament. I'd like to give it to your Uncle Norval to take with him. I hope that's all right with you. Your mother will give you another one." She spoke quietly and somewhat pained. I was still not fully awake, but I muttered it was all right. The full import of grandmother's request didn't sink in until the next day. I realized it was because of her concern for the welfare of Uncle Norval. I had helped her as she saw it to bring God's protection to bear. I, a teenager, had made a contribution to the adult world of anxiety in respect to survival in a war-torn world.

As it turned out, neither of my uncles left the United States. Uncle Norval was assigned to a military post on Staten Island, NY, from which soldiers were shipped for service throughout the world. Often servicemen's farewell parties prior to departure took place in Manhattan bars. My husky 38-year-old uncle was a military policeman. He and a companion were assigned the task of taking a ferry to Manhattan, entering bars and removing drunken soldiers so they would be on their assigned ships the next day. Uncle Norval was mustered out of the army with honorable discharge September 7, 1945. My two uncles saw military service but were never directly involved in battlefront operations.

Uncle Wellington (Tom) Taylor was also a vocational agriculture teacher which meant that he was not called up quickly. He taught at Summerville, MO, High School and was married to Dortha with one son Teddy when drafted. He was 27 when he was inducted May 23, 1945, and mustered out December 28, 1945, four months after Japan surrendered. When he completed basic training he was sent to Fort Riley near Manhattan, Kansas. He served as his company's clerk while the rest of those with whom he did basic were sent overseas. Admired older mentors were taken from among us but we endured; giving up close relatives in a sense was our contribution to the war effort.

The Taylor family did have one casualty. Aunt Bertha, who was then teaching home economics near Kansas City, at age 41 married a fellow teacher John C. Seuell on September 25, 1942. He was a 1st Lieutenant and I was around him a few days after they were married. I recall him always wearing his uniform. Those days too comprised most of the contact the rest of the family had with John. He shipped out of New York for Europe and on February 7, 1943, the German U-402 sank his ship the Henry R. Mallory not too far from Greenland, killing 272 Americans.

TROOP MOVEMENTS

Soon after the beginning of the war uniformed men and equipment became increasingly obvious in southern Missouri. The railroads grew increasingly important. Thayer, founded as a rail center located between Springfield, Missouri, and Memphis, Tennessee, was of considerable importance because of its roundhouse. Because of a turntable of up to 120 feet, engines and other cars, when necessary, could be turned around and used to pull trains heading in the opposite direction. During war time the Frisco railway, that is, the Saint Louis and San Francisco, running through Thayer, was a main line between Kansas City, Missouri, and Birmingham, Alabama. At its peak 400 employees of Frisco worked out of the Thayer rail yards. Soon about every passenger train contained troops being transferred. I seldom went downtown myself, but my friends told of purchasing candy bars, cold drinks, and comic books and selling them to the soldiers through the train windows in their twenty-minute stops to let passengers on and off. As the war progressed freight trains carried military vehicles, large field artillery guns, and tanks.

Highway 63 entering Missouri from Iowa ran through Columbia, Jefferson City, West Plains, Thayer, and on to West Memphis. Highway 19 ran south from Hannibal through Alton to Thayer. As the war peaked convoys constantly occupied the highways. They tended to move somewhat slower than the other traffic and left gaps between vehicles so that civilian traffic could weave in and out. Because of a wartime universal 35-mile speed limit all the vehicles seemed to move at a snail's pace. We observed all manner of military vehicles, some pulling equipment loaded on trailers. Our house just south of Thayer was on highway 63, as was our grandparents' an additional half mile south. We liked to watch the convoys. It was almost as exciting as a parade, and exhibited constant variety. When our apples were ripe my brothers, Glenn and Owen, stood near the highway and tossed apples from our orchard to the soldiers. The GIs seemed unusually grateful. Occasionally conveys halted, and uniformed men hastened to my grandfather's store purchasing candy, cold drinks, bananas, and other edibles

One of the reasons for troop movements was that Fort Leonard Wood in Waynesville, Missouri, became one of the largest army bases in the United States with above 50,000 troops at the height of the war. It served as a major training center preparing troops for overseas deployment. Ground breaking on Fort Leonard Wood began December 5, 1940. The first troops arrived in May 1941, before the war began. The building of the base impacted even our region for two or three years even though the camp was 130 miles north. My grandfather's business grew exponentially because of the employment of carpenters and other laborers who traveled north out of Arkansas to construct the Fort. Men who left their families at home drove to Fort Leonard Wood on Sunday afternoon and returned home after work on Friday. My grandfather extended the hours of his gas station and food store so as to accommodate the traveling workers. My grandfather was an entrepreneur for the time and place. He kept bologna and American cheese in large chunks, and he always had Holsum brand bread readily available. He made sandwiches with bologna and cheese hand sliced as thick as the traveling workers desired, charging by the weight. I recall some ordering pieces an inch thick. He had mustard and catsup available. He also sold plenty of cookies, nuts, apples, oranges, and bananas. Because of the expanding camp, the construction continued for more than a year.

DAYLIGHT SAVINGS TIME

Other aspects of daily living changed. Noticeable to students my age was daylight savings time. The Roosevelt administration enacted year-round-daylight savings time from February 9, 1942 to September 30, 1945. Daylight savings time was enforced for a time in World War I, but was not popular. Because of the emergency situation in WWII it was accepted, if sometimes begrudgedly, for the good of the cause. This meant that in the winter we got up in the dark to go to school, and after school a little time was left to play outside. We liked daylight savings time in the summer. My brothers and I relished getting up early because our parents and grandparents always rose about 6 A.M. Our day was therefore expanded because we could play tag, hide and seek, catch, softball, and football in the summer until 9 P.M.

Surprisingly, soon after the war began we had black outs. It seems unlikely that we would have been bombed, but then Thayer was a vital railroad center. We had to buy heavy-duty cloth blinds for our windows. When the regulation went into effect officials in the city traveled throughout the town and area to make sure little light was visible. They flew over the city at night to further pinpoint any excessive light. I recall thinking how black our rooms had became, a nightly reminder of the war.

RATIONING, PRICE CONTROL, AND RECYCLING

Another new development in the war impacted our life, but especially the running of grandfather's store. That was rationing. At the same time, however, because of our connection with the store and our limited needs we were little deprived. Early in 1942, rationing went into effect and rationing books were issued. All this meant considerable book keeping in our little store but we coped. Larger items were rationed, such as cars, refrigerators, stoves, and tires. Few cars and household items were manufactured during the war since all the effort went toward building tanks, airplanes, and ships. Gasoline and tires were rationed along with sugar, coffee, butter, meat, fish, milk, shoes, and nylons.

War

Most people in small towns depended minimally on stamps for food supplies because they produced meat and milk products themselves and all sorts of vegetables, nuts, and fruit. One item at a premium was sugar, especially cane sugar. Beet sugar was manufactured before the war, but mostly used in canned foods. It became available in stores after the war began. We sold beet sugar, but most of our customers prized cane sugar. One time my grandfather received a large shipment of beet sugar in ten pound bags. We stacked it on palettes on the north side of the store. It took longer to sell than we anticipated. Various people gave my grandfather sugar stamps they didn't need, so that he could pass them on to others. Saccharin, which was available in small pills, had been in production since early in the twentieth century and now was widely used in coffee and cooking. Butter was never scarce in our family or with many in the small towns, but margarine or oleo became available and was widely used. Rationing was much more important in larger cities even though victory gardens became popular. Nylons, however, were scarce. Women either went without stockings or wore rayon or cotton ones.

Most people were not compelled to drive far in our region, so gas and tire rationing was not as constricting as elsewhere. My grandfather always had extra gasoline stamps available for anyone who needed them. My father seldom used his allotted amount. My Uncle Cleo had to travel more than some to visit farmers, and he needed gasoline for his farming operations; but he never had to go without. When it was clear that gas rationing was to go into effect Uncle Cleo bought a 55 gallon oil drum from Uncle Norval, built a stand for it so it could lay on its side for easy withdrawal, and filled it with gasoline. The gasoline sat in this reserved barrel for the duration of the war. When gas rationing was lifted Uncle Cleo decided to burn it in his tractor mixed with post-war gasoline. But the aged gasoline caused the motor to lose so much power that he concluded that he should dispose of it. The stored gasoline only cost about 10 cents a gallon. During the war the price of gasoline was frozen at 14 cents a gallon.

Efforts were made to collect scrap metal, aluminum cans, tires, and paper for recycling. My grandfather set aside a part of the field on the north side of his house along the highway so persons could drop off items for later collection. Most of the items left were either scrap iron or tires. Collection was more readily attained than pick up. After awhile it was necessary to stack the tires in a high mound reaching ten feet. It was almost a year before someone who removed such materials hauled them away, forcing us to question the advisability of their collection. The irregular collection may have resulted from our isolation and rather small amounts compared with that around large cities.

SOCIAL ACTIVITIES

In the families, life went on normally except for missing key members. My mother's extended family continued to gather at my grandparents every Sunday and major holidays. As I entered the teenage years the United States was fully engaged in war in Europe and the Pacific. Activities were somewhat limited for teenagers. The main gathering place for teenagers other than high school was at the picture show. Alton, Missouri, hovered at 500 inhabitants during the war. The movie house, which seated 120, was in an older remodeled building on the southeast corner of the court house square on highway 160 leaving town. As I recall movies were shown Thursday through Saturday nights with a matinee on Saturday afternoon. I was not aware of teenagers meeting at the picture shows as a group, but no doubt some did, but mostly girls with girls and boys with boys at my age. By age 15 or 16 a few couples around Alton started to date.

Most of the movies revolved about military conflicts or westerns. My uncle and aunt never went to the movies. After I arrived at Alton in 1943 I was only permitted to attend the Saturday afternoon matinees which were entirely westerns. I loved westerns, which at the matinee cost $.25. With every movie was a news reel of 10 to 15 minutes which mostly gave an update on the progress of the war. I recall numerous reels depicting air battles and bombings, ships firing aircraft weapons at planes, PT boats landing on Pacific islands, and tanks under Patton rumbling across North Africa. At times other than Saturday we constantly had work to complete. Most Saturday afternoons my uncle drove up to the square, got out, and made his way around conversing with farmers regarding crops and problems. Part of his position as a vocational agriculture teacher was to be in contact with farmers, and visiting on the square was an important means of engaging in personal conversations. Most farmers came into town on Saturday afternoon to purchase feed, seed, fertilizers, tools, and equipment. Their wives came with them to shop and acquire the needed groceries. Part of that time those who came in from the country sat on benches or the low walls around the court house talking with friends and exchanging information about crops, soil conditions, and animals. Their children, if they came to town, likely attended the matinee. These afternoon western movies normally featured in addition, a western serial; some of the names attached to the serials that I remember were Tom Mix and Wild Bill Hickok. Some of the serials were older reruns. Various people starred in westerns, but my favorites were Gene Autry and Roy Rogers. I liked the Autry movies somewhat better because I loved the western songs he sang and tried to emulate his voice. By singing his songs over and over I memorized several of them. The songs weren't always integrated into the script, but I didn't mind because I was normally more into the songs than the script anyway. I usually attended the movies by myself, though I saw classmates there on occasion. After the war I attended two or three times with a date.

Another place that appealed to some teenagers was the drugstore where one could purchase cherry cokes, ice cream sodas, sundaes, and chocolate malted shakes. It also had a side room that had two or three pinball machines. After school I often walked to my uncle's house about three-quarters of a mile east from the high school. Teachers usually stayed around school an hour after the students left for meetings and putting classrooms in order. On the way home I started stopping at the drug store to play a purely mechanical pinball machine. I got pretty good at my favorite one and spent little money because I kept winning free games. After awhile, however, my aunt told me that I was to walk straight home and not stop at the drug store. She thought it not appropriate that I spend time there. Perhaps she perceived it as a pool hall where, so some thought, good Christians did not enter. Pool halls were declared to be a waste of time and encouraged foul and vulgar language as well as beer drinking. None of my high school peers as far as I knew frequented pool halls.

The other activities for teenagers revolved largely around the schools. The main activity was sports. Sports were limited during the war. Alton High School offered two sports in high school competition, basketball for boys and volleyball for girls. We played other schools in Missouri and northern Arkansas, but mostly schools in our Oregon County league, consisting of Alton, Couch, Koshkonong, and Thomasville. The other high school in the county was at Thayer but it was in the South Central Missouri conference which featured football. The high schools in the SCA were Thayer, West Plains, Willow Springs, Cabool, and Mountain Grove. All the high schools bussed in students from the countryside. Alton transported students from the northeast part of the county, the longest distances which required above an hour one way. Alton had the highest attendance in the county of about

230 students, which grew to 250 after the war was over. The next in order of size in Oregon County were Thayer, Couch, Koshkonong, and Thomasville. But size didn't determine the conference winners. Alton often came in first in girl's volleyball, but not usually in basketball. I often preferred watching the girls play because they were excellent and usually won.

The basketball/volleyball nights were major community gatherings and many people packed the gymnasium. Games normally took place on Tuesday and Thursday nights. Older students might arrange a date for the games, but normally groups of boys and girls sat together in the bleachers. Our FFA club sold soft drinks and candy bars, and I was often involved with the selling. Early in the war it was decided that it took up too much gasoline for individual cars to travel out of town for games. So the school board decided to make a bus or two available. At most, the distances were 25 miles one way. Students paid, as I recall, fifty cents for the ride. Riders on the bus grouped with friends sometimes consisting of both boys and girls. After a time or two I and four or five other students, perhaps three girls and two fellows, sat in the back of the bus and sang religious songs, mostly of the Stamps-Baxter variety. We were from different backgrounds, Baptist, Methodist and I, Church of Christ. After a few rides our theme song became, "He Set me Free," first published by Albert E. Brumley, of Powell, Missouri, in 1939. We sang other of Brumley's songs, "I'll Fly Away," and "I'll Meet You in the Morning." Though we became singing friends we never paired off. Two of the singers were a brother and sister.

We had high school outings, but not at great distances. When I was a freshman the class went on an outing to Greer Springs, a defunct old feed mill located about ten miles northeast of Alton. The unique water wheel was down about 500 feet in a canyon. The considerable flow of dammed-up water out of the spring traveled to the Eleven Point River, a mile to the north. The water wheel was in a structure by the dam. The mill itself was on level ground near highway 19 about ¾ of a mile distant from the spring. The power from the water wheel was transferred to the mill above by a continuous steel cable running around wheels about two feet in diameter. Our whole class walked down to the bottom then back up on an undeveloped trail sometimes with small ditches and a few rocks. I walked down and back with a sister and brother, Betty and Billy Millsap. On the way back Betty sometimes wanted help so I extended my hand to help her over rough spots. She seemed attracted to me, and I talked with her some, but we never became romantically involved. She was more interested in me than I her.

War

Another favorite spot for an outing was the Grand Gulf about ten miles west of Thayer. The gulf was caused by the collapse of a natural roof over an underground river. Such a formation was unusual in that it produced a gulf of about a mile long with side arms of some yards in length. The gulf lay about 150 feet deep below ground level. Sinkholes covered this Ozark region. Sinkholes likewise resulted from cave-ins in which limestone eroded underneath over long periods of time, and then the ceiling collapsed. But few if any other cave-ins resulted in lengthy gulfs. It was then surmised in 1943 that water in the gulf, which disappeared into a cavern on one end, ended up in the large Mammoth Spring some 15 miles away in Arkansas. The re-emergence of the water at Mammoth Spring was later proven through placing hay bales in the stream at the gulf. They later showed up in Mammoth Spring. For this sophomore outing we traveled to the site in a couple of school buses and spent most of the day. We walked around and down into the gulf, over and under a natural bridge, had a picnic lunch, and returned home in time for the end of the school day. A couple or two may have paired off, but I don't recall that many did. Some of the churches had youth groups, but I didn't know much about them. The Churches of Christ we attended in Thayer and Mammoth had some teenagers, but no effort was made to bring them together for either teaching or social occasions.

Soon after I arrived in Alton I learned that some of the mothers decided to create gatherings at their houses for the mixing of what they perceived as the desirable youth in Alton. About twenty were invited with an equal number of boys and girls. We played games in backyards. These may have resulted in pairing, some of which became permanent. After I went off to Harding College (now University) in 1947, I didn't keep up with who may have married whom. The girls I knew about tended to marry somewhat older men from an earlier class. Jack Holman, a classmate, married a girl in our class immediately after graduation. Unfortunately Jack, who was outstanding in the hundred yard dash, developed leg cancer and died within a year after his marriage. I was paired in these gatherings with Helen Dorris. Her father, Gordon Dorris, was a circuit judge in four southern Missouri counties and a neighbor to Uncle Cleo when he first started teaching at Alton. I liked her, and we talked occasionally. After I turned sixteen I asked her for a movie date. She informed me that her father would not let her date as yet. She was fifteen. I never got up the courage to ask her again. As far as I knew she had not dated anyone when I went off to Harding.

MISSOURI MEMORIES, 1934–1947

RANCHING IN MISSOURI

I myself did not have many opportunities for pastimes, and most of my peers who also lived on farms were similarly occupied. Others who didn't live on farms often worked. My cousin James Ray Dunsmore started shining shoes in his father's barber shop. My uncle was very busy both teaching and farming. Our usual day was to get up a six A.M. We milked about twenty cows. When I first went to stay with my uncle we supplied half-pint bottled milk for the government-supported school milk program. We had to maintain certain standards for scalding the bottles. One of my cousins, Bertha Prewitt, stayed with my uncle and aunt and helped with the milking and bottling. We also delivered milk in quart bottles to people in town. Later, we stopped delivery in town and started selling milk in ten gallon steel cans to a cheese factory in West Plains. At night after I got home from school I took the returned milk cans up the hill, now filled with whey, which was the liquid remaining after milk has been curdled and strained at the cheese plant. After changing clothes I "slopped" the pigs by adding ground corn to the whey. Slop was any food stuff humans preferred not to eat such as potato peels and table scraps and whey. As additional chores I fed hay to the cows, sheep, and goats. In birthing seasons we kept constant watch on the lambs, piglets, and kids. I also fed the chickens and gathered eggs in a new chicken house on the upper level of the hog house. Almost the whole day was consumed with school and farm activities. In the gardening season, April through September, I worked in the large garden. We were usually free after about 7:30 P.M. Uncle Cleo listened to the news of the war and especially the farm and farm market reports of various kinds. He did this not only for informing his students and the farmers, but to enhance his own farm operations. Summer activities on the farm took up the time vacated when school ceased. We understood that our efforts to provide food and hard work contributed to the war effort. Perhaps what we did was not much, but we did what we could. We worked constantly and used our time as wisely as possible.

 School ended in the middle of May and then we started our summer's work. Not long before I moved to Alton my uncle bought a thousand acres that commenced a mile south of the Alton town line. The land was hilly and rocky and covered with scrub brush, because all the suitable timber had been cut perhaps twenty years before. A few cleared fields existed, enough to provide some pasture. My uncle decided to reduce the brush by establishing a herd of about a hundred goats. He didn't want just any goats since he knew about the profitability of Angora goats. Because of the scarcity of fibers during the war wool was in demand and Angora goats produced mohair twice a year. We had to keep a watch on the goats because as their hair got longer they sometimes got it caught in bushes and fences. At least once a week we walked the fence rows and other areas frequented by the goats to release goats that became entangled. We often found one or two. We sheared the goats ourselves, but usually when school was going on, so we had to work nights. My uncle was interested in riding horses and went to Tennessee with his stock trailer and bought a Tennessee Walking Horse. The horse was beautifully colored and would have been an expensive horse were it not for a defective hip. My uncle always wanted me to ride "Ole Smokey," but I didn't really care that much for horses. I had rather run, and I could make it through the bush and rocks as fast on foot as I could on Smokey. But Uncle Cleo insisted that I take him because Smokey needed to be ridden. He was a horse with a head of his own and, at least for me, difficult to control. He liked to head for the nearest tree and wipe me off his back. He and I therefore fought over how near he was permitted to trees.

We spent considerable time building fences to keep the animals in more manageable locations. We also had beef cattle, a herd of 50 or more on the ranch, on which we also kept an eye. At the start of winter we drove the cattle through town on a side road to the sixty-acre farm on which Uncle Cleo lived east of Alton. We fed them hay, cotton seed meal, and some grain. Because of the feeding it was much more convenient to have them close at hand. As the pastures began to grow in March we drove them in a herd back to the ranch since they no longer needed to be fed. We also looked over the cattle for any problems at the same time as we searched out the goats.

During World War I my grandfather bought feeder livestock for resale at the major markets until the early twenties when he settled down at the gas station. He mainly bought feeder hogs and cattle from farmers so as to transport them by train to St. Louis or Kansas City. At these major stockyards the grain farmers in Northern Missouri and Illinois purchased by auction grandfather's feeder stock. It was common for the farmers of our region to raise pigs and cattle and sell them when they reached young adulthood, pigs at six months and cattle at a year. They could raise them to this age feeding them little grain. The pigs ate acorns in the woods and the calves ate grass and dead leaves from the bushes in the winter supplemented with a modicum of hay and cotton seed. Grandfather would collect the animals he bought on his small farm northeast of Thayer until he had enough to make a shipment. The northern famers who grew large amounts of corn, wheat, barley, and oats fattened them up for three months and put them on the market, ready for slaughter. My grandfather did well, but it took him away from home more than he liked. I loved to hear his stories about riding in the caboose of the same train as his livestock. Other buyers were often on the train and they played cards to occupy the time. One of grandfather's favorite stories was the time the trainmen in St. Louis made a mistake and their train was long on its way to Chicago before they noticed the miscue.

At the beginning of World War II, Uncle Cleo followed in his father's footsteps and bought feeders toward fall and sold them to grain farmers in northwest Missouri normally around Maryville, MO, but he didn't need to accompany the livestock to the markets on trains. By now livestock trucks were common, and the animals could be directly transported from my Uncle's feeder lots to a specific farmer in the north. Uncle Cleo was an inveterate bargainer and purchased the stock for as little as possible, sometimes to the wonderment of the Oregon County farmers. As his own farm operations increased, however, he ceased purchasing livestock for immediate resale.

By the time school was out, hay was ready to be cut. In 1943 Uncle Cleo purchased the first pickup hay baler to be owned in Oregon County. He ordered it and had to wait some time for delivery, since it was war time and a limited number of balers were being built. Prior to that time Oregon County balers were stationary, and hay had to be hauled, usually on horse drawn wagons, to the baler. He also purchased his first tractor, a Ford Ferguson, which the Ford Motor Company started to build in 1938. It was a smaller tractor but highly useful because it had a hydraulic lift system. By this time Uncle Cleo was growing alfalfa on granddad Taylor's farm, eventually occupying about twenty acres. I was present and involved the first time the baler was used in the alfalfa field south of the Taylor gas station. It took four persons to operate the baler: a tractor driver, a person to feed the hay into the hopper, and two persons to tie the bales. The person feeding the hay stood on a high platform and therefore could oversee the whole operation. The two persons tying the bales sat on a wooden bench with a wooden platform for their feet that ran the length of the baler. A block two inches thick and about 14 X12 inches separated the bales. The block was injected into the baler by a mechanism when the hopper was clean of hay. The one feeding the baler determined the time of injection by a device that pushed it down when the compactor came down. That plunger was synchronized with the main horizontal plunger that compressed the hay. The block had grooves on each side about two inches from the top and the bottom. When those tying the bales saw the block coming they pushed a wire through the groove to the other side. The wire was precut to length and had a twisted eye. The person on the other side pushed the wire back through the next block. Then the first person took the straight end, put it through the eye, and wrapped the wire around three or four times so as to tie the two wires at the top and bottom of the bale. One had to be focused and fairly fast to wire the bales as they came through. As each bale came out the end of the baler the block had to be caught and returned to the feeder. On that first day I sat on one side of the baler to help tie the bales. I was a bit awkward at first, but soon got the hang of it. No one on our crew had worked on a baler before, but Uncle Cleo had observed many stationary balers and had seen this one demonstrated.

Uncle Cleo also purchased a side delivery rake. All the rakes I had seen before were dump rakes. We had one and pulled it with horses. I was given the job a time or two but did not relish it, for it was difficult for me to control the horses and at the same time dump at the right place in order to make straight windrows. I never learned to appreciate horses. They seemed to dominate me rather than I them. I was always amazed at how Albert Prewitt could keep them under control. The side delivery rake piled the hay to the side so that the rows always flowed in such a manner that they could easily be followed by the pickup baler even around corners.

Uncle Cleo was a friend of the wealthiest man in Alton, Ben Gum, who was president of the Alton bank and who owned the Ford Agency, the only auto agency in town. Ben sold far more pickups than cars. My Uncle did not own a car all the way through the war. A pickup was far more useful for his various enterprises. Most persons with pickups had their names painted on the door by a professional painter. Uncle Cleo had 'Cleo S. Taylor' painted on the two front doors of his pickup. Even Gum drove a pickup with 'Ben M. Gum' on it. Gum owned a large river-bottom farm near Billmore about twenty miles southeast of Alton. As one traveled east toward the rivers, the land flattened out, was less rocky and more fertile than in our region. When Uncle Cleo bought the pickup baler in the third year of the war he not only baled his own hay, but took on baling jobs for other farmers, charging 5 cents a bale. We moved our equipment to the Gum farm one afternoon so as to bale his hay the next day. Gum had two or three families living on the farm taking care of the operations. No doubt after the war Gum purchased his own pickup baler, but farm equipment was difficult to acquire during the war. By 1944 I, at age 15, ran the baling crew which consisted of my two brothers and another young man my age named Johnny Allen. Johnny drove the tractor, I fed the hay into the baler from the chute bringing it up from the ground, and my brothers, Glenn and Owen, tied the bales. Owen was 12 and not fully grown yet.

    The day arrived for us to start baling. It was a nice sunny day. My uncle took us down in the pickup and made sure everything was ready to go, then left. Ben Gum was there too, for the start. There were four men standing around waiting to put the hay in the barn as soon at it was baled. Since we were charging by the bale Ben wanted to put as much hay in each bale as was possible. After we had made a round he decided the bales could be heavier so he screwed the back end of the baler down so the bales weighed at least 70 pounds. When the men first saw our baling crew they thought they would have a relaxing day. They laughed and asked us if we thought we could keep them busy. We said we didn't know, but we thought so. The hay was red top, a native grass and rather easy to bale. We started about 10 A.M. so all signs of dew would be gone. Ben Gum left when we were well into the swing of things. After the first hour one of the men came and implored us to lighten the bales. He said they were too heavy. We didn't mind so we opened up the screws on the baler so that the bales weighed between 50 and 60 pounds.

    We were not much given to taking breaks, but we did stop to drink water occasionally and eat a bit of candy. At noon the whole crew, us included, ate at the main farm table. The farm had a dug well about 90 feet deep which was unusual for a dug well. The water drawn from the well in a bucket was cold and outstanding. The food was good, and dinner (i. e. lunch) was the main meal of the day. One of the farmers had a daughter a year older than I and some of the farm hands kidded me about her. She wasn't bad looking, but we didn't have much time to talk. Owen, my youngest brother, was always hungry and often asked how long it would be until meal time. We started designating him "dinner bell." About the middle of the afternoon one of the men came over to the baler and asked if we couldn't take a break. He pointed out they had to stack all the bales in the barn that night, and we were killing them we were racking up so many. We said we were supposed to keep going. We baled until about seven that night and turned out 714 bales according to the counter on the baler. The farm hands would likely be another two hours putting all the bales in the barn. On the way home we decided it served them right because they laughed at our crew in respect to what we might accomplish.

Some argued that growing up a teenager in the midst of World War II was the worst of times. We seemed to be restricted on all fronts. Food and consumer goods were limited. Travel was constricted. Families were scattered either because of military service or working in plants manufacturing war equipment and supplies. But for me these were great boot camp years for life ahead. My Uncle would have employed more mature persons had they been available, but they were scattered on many fronts. That enabled me to step in. I learned discipline through having several reoccurring responsibilities, chores we called them. My uncle taught me not only how to do various jobs and the need to do them as best as I could, but how to manage time and achieve much in a short order. He also taught me the need to know what was happening in the world so as to be able to respond to the trends and fluctuations. He stressed that one had to cope with the world heads up. Knowledge and education were extremely desirable. As it turned out I never took up farming, but the principles I learned have served me well as a college professor and administrator.

Chapter IX

Peace

The invasion of Normandy Beach, D-Day, occurred June 6, 1944, two years and a half after the United States entered the war. It was a long time coming. We had been confident from the beginning that we would ultimately win, but numerous setbacks were reported nightly by newscaster Lowell Thomas. Finally the amazing news of the long orchestrated and executed Normandy invasion broke, and we knew we were on the way to victory. D-Day was not V-Day, but the war could never be visualized in the same manner again after this famous beach landing. We knew many battles were yet to be fought in Europe and the Pacific. Sherman tanks, commanded by General Patton, still had to rumble across France, and commanders of PT boats for example, John F. Kennedy, still had to attack the beaches of South Sea Islands. But signs of ultimate victory constantly emerged as the weeks flew past. Finally, in late April 1945 the Nazis started to crumble, and surrender documents were prepared.

In late July of 1945 the focus was on Japan. The territory they occupied was constantly shrinking. On August 6, 1945, the amazing news broke that atomic bombs, about which we had heard rumors, were dropped on Hiroshima and Nagasaki. The Thayer Church of Christ was having a Gospel Meeting. I had gone down to stay with my parents a few days so as to attend. I arrived early, so I was walking around the grounds of the Thayer Elementary School from which I had graduated. Suddenly the town sirens burst forth. These were sounded every day at noon, intensifying, then subsiding. The sirens also heralded a major fire and pierced the air every November 11 at 11 A.M. on Armistice Day to celebrate the ending of World War I. I didn't know what the sirens that August day signified, so I wandered back over to the church building and was informed of the atomic bombs and that it was anticipated that Japan would soon surrender. Peace had finally arrived after four long years!

WAR STORIES

Change was not immediate, but gradually arrived. Rationing was wound down and price controls lifted. Soldiers returned from the front. Some wanted to share incidents from the battles, but others wanted to quickly and silently get back to their shops and farms. I never heard my highly decorated cousin Albert describe any of his exploits. Most of my relatives were the silent type. My cousin Bertha Prewitt, Albert's sister, married Ned Johnson a year before the war ended, and he liked to talk, too much for my father's pleasure. Dad called him a windbag. Ned was a tail gunner on a B17 bomber. He reported that one time after a bombing raid over Germany they were attacked by a squadron of German Messerschmitts. The fighting was prolonged and vicious. After awhile Ned ran out of ammunition. He was in an exposed position and perplexed as to what to do. He saw some paper stacked nearby. It dawned on him that small pieces of paper flowing out the rear of the plane would appear as a stream of bullets. He quickly tore up several large handfuls and threw them out a window in the turret. He was delighted to discover that the attacking fighter plane feigned left and right as if the paper bits were a stream of bullets to dodge. It was a good story, but some of my relatives doubted its veracity. They remarked that Ned was a good story teller.

We heard other amazing stories. Few farm structures were built during the war for lack of materials and manpower. In 1946 my uncle decided to construct a large shed to house farm equipment and vehicles. At that time he didn't have a garage. He employed a carpenter, Louis Simpson, to build it. I helped Louis after school and on Saturdays. Louis liked to talk when he worked, mostly about construction in which he was involved during the war. My father built rental houses on lots he owned because a new demand for housing opened up after the war. My brothers and I sometimes helped, and we liked to talk while we worked. Dad would sometimes look at us with a scowl and in a demanding voice declare, "Don't talk—work." We also sang a lot when we worked. Dad was somewhat more open to singing.

I heard many wartime stories from Louis. He was in his early fifties and hadn't served in the war but had worked on major military projects. He was an excellent carpenter. In 1943 he heard of a significant demand for construction workers in Hanford, Washington, in an isolated area on the Columbia River. The pay was excellent, and workers were required for a number of months. He loaded up his pickup and left his family in Missouri since little housing was available and headed to Hanford. The workmen in the Hanford crew in which Louis worked learned that they would not be told the reason for the buildings on which they were working. The construction required high security. Of course, the secrecy did not restrict speculation about what it might be. The structures were identified as the Hanford Project, but it was unknown by the workers that their buildings were related to the famous Manhattan Project for producing the atomic bomb. The Hanford facility was constructed for the explicit purpose of converting uranium to plutonium. The workers had a difficult time even envisioning structures such as these. In some areas walls were poured ten feet thick. Little of their labor made sense to them. The large number of construction workers on the site also stretched credibility of the crew, at times up to 50,000 persons. It was not until after the dropping of the bombs on Hiroshima and Nagasaki that the employees learned to their great surprise the purpose of what their construction facilitated. Louis told me other wartime construction stories, but the Hanford Project was the most memorable.

FUTURE FARMERS OF AMERICA

Part of my school life centered in the FFA (Future Farmers of America) chapter at Alton High. We were active during the war and held regular meetings. I was elected to various offices, eventually becoming president. Some of my peers thought I was a shoo-in since Uncle Cleo was the sponsor. Before the war the chapter had an annual encampment in the middle of the summer in some remote area. These were discontinued during the war. My Uncle liked these outings and the esprit de corps they created. He, therefore, announced at the close of school in 1946 that we would have a summer encampment on the Eleven Point River about six miles above Riverton east of Alton on highway 160.

Our encampment was scheduled for late July since farm activities started to slow down after plowing, planting, and haying ceased. I helped gather all the supplies in our pickup. A few of the older boys had vehicles, and off we went in a caravan. The activity was an overnighter. We arrived at the camp site about five PM in time to build a fire and roast wieners and marshmallows. Following the meal we had time for a baseball game. As it grew dark we sat around the fire, talking, telling stories, and reminiscing about the activities of the 1946–47 school year. The long -time tradition was that no one was permitted to sleep, though those monitoring were self appointed. Persons normally tried to sleep on or near the camp site so that the likelihood of getting in a few winks was minimal. Two of my friends and I decided we didn't want to stay up all night, so on the way in we looked for a place to sleep where we wouldn't be disturbed. About a mile from the site we noticed a barn with a hayloft and plenty of hay. We concluded that sleeping on hay would be ideal, and the others wouldn't know where to find us. Toward midnight we started getting sleepy, so we told our classmates that we needed to wake up so we were going for a walk. Our plans were not to return so we headed one way then circled back toward the barn. We didn't have a flashlight, just matches. We climbed up to the hay loft but knew enough not to light matches for fear of setting the hay afire. I climbed up a ways on a mound of hay looking for a good place to lie down. Almost immediately I felt a significant sting below the nail of my thumb on my left hand. I asked someone to light a match. We didn't see anything in the hay but my thumb was marked by two dots of blood, clearly fang marks. We didn't know what sort of snake it was, but likely because of the marks a poisonous snake, hopefully not a rattler. We decided that the only thing to do was walk back to the camp and report the bite to Uncle Cleo. By time we arrived the arm had begun to swell. Uncle Cleo immediately took out his knife, cut slits on the fang marks and began to suck. The standard country procedure then was to suck on the wound under the supposition that the venom would be drawn out. Such was generally believed, but later studies failed to support this remedy. We concluded that the snake was probably a copperhead of which plenty were around. We decided that no need existed to return to town until after daylight since the doctor wouldn't be available until 8 AM. Our scheme to sleep that night was ruined. We planned to leave about 6:30 in the morning, however, so as to be first in line at the doctor's office. When we started back to town my arm was swollen all the way to my shoulder. It was a good encampment, but for me, at least, a painful ending. The doctor told me to put rubbing alcohol on the arm and the swelling would go down in a few days.

Another tradition of our FFA was a trip to the American Royal Livestock Show in Kansas City. The American Royal was founded in 1899. FFA was founded at a Royal gathering in 1928. Uncle Cleo had taken FFA members on annual trips there from the middle 1930s when he started teaching at Alton. The Royal was either closed down or much reduced during World War II. The national FFA organization met during the war with only a few delegates. Now once again the Alton FFA club was returning to the expanded American Royal in the fall of 1946. Uncle Cleo arranged to take a school bus. He drove the bus himself. We took as many members as wished to go. As I recall we had about twenty making the trip. We each paid some of the expenses, and some money was taken from the chapter treasury. We stayed at the YMCA in Kansas City. Several could stay in a single barracks-like room at a very reasonable cost.

We geared up for the trip with great excitement. Most of us had traveled little during the war and few of us as far as Kansas City. The farthest I had been away from home was Poplar Bluff, Missouri, ninety miles east of Alton. I, as yet, at age 16, had not seen a traffic light. I saw my first traffic light in Springfield on the way to Kansas City. Kansas City was a major city in my eyes with over 400,000 people. We neared the city as night began to fall. The lights on the horizon exceeded my imagination.

Our first responsibility was to attend the official meetings of FFA. I was selected as the delegate for our club with the privilege of commenting or making motions. About 500 delegates assembled in a large tiered auditorium, the largest gathering in which I had ever been involved. Being somewhat reticent I observed without asking to speak. I was impressed with the efficiency with which my peers from other schools carried on the business.

In between the FFA sessions we visited the livestock exhibits. We had already experienced livestock competitions at regional fairs that had started up again after the war. Our chapter had a judging team, and Uncle Cleo asked us to fill out a form in which we rated the animals: milk cows, beef cattle, horses, hogs, sheep, goats, chickens, ducks, and rabbits. Later, when the decisions of the judges were posted on the pens, we could compare our decisions with theirs. The exhibits at the Royal were far more extensive and of better quality than any we experienced at the county fairs. We were able to observe varieties of animals of which we had seen pictures in books, but never in reality. In two years after our visit the American Royal incorporated a rodeo into the week's activities. We were familiar with rodeos, since before the war Thayer leaders promoted a rodeo which took place on the

Arden Risner farm east of the Warm Fork. We marveled over a horse show at the Royal. The horses were put through various paces. The acts included jumping and running in tandem, a rider with a foot on each.

Kansas City held other major attractions. Toward the Missouri river we visited the tremendous Kansas City stockyards as well as packing plants. In the stockyards we strode on high wooden walkways above the pens and observed all sorts of animals awaiting purchase by the packing plants. Inside the packing plants we also walked on high runways above where cows were killed by a straight forward shot in the brain, and sheep and hogs were hanging by their legs while workers came along and slit their throats with a sharp knife. The weather by now was cool but there was a warm sickening smell in the rendering plant from the blood and manure. Afterward we visited the meat storage, cutting, and packaging area. It was cooler and smelled of cold locker meat.

By the fall of 1946 domestic auto production boomed in the United States. Few cars were built during the war. A major General Motors assembling plant stood near the Fairfax Airport in Kansas City. As the war wound down a large facility occupied the spot for the construction of B25 bombers. By the time we visited, workmen in three shifts were turning out Chevrolet Cars in the same facility. The assembly lines were long, and it was amazing to stand on walkways above and view the process. We were able to walk from the beginning to the end of the assembly line.

My class at Alton had twin brothers, John and Joe Barton. I became a good friend of John Barton. John thought he and I should also be educated in the ways of the world, so he located a burlesque house and kept after me until I agreed to go with him to a show. We were able to get away because free times were in the schedule for us to visit the city on our own. I don't know what my uncle would have thought of our visit. We didn't dare ask. I had heard my rather staid aunt, however, Bertha Taylor, a home economics teacher, talk about having seen Sally Rand on stage. She thought Rand's fan dance was an art and to be admired.

We arrived at the burlesque house, I with fear and trepidation. One was supposed to be 18 to purchase a ticket, but apparently the rule was very lax since we were not asked for identification. I think we may have been asked if we 18, and if so, we lied. They sold us the tickets. I grew more relaxed after the first skits which were burlesque routines and dance numbers. Some of the language was risqué and also the references, but not nearly as straight forward and suggestive as present-day TV comedy shows. There were some dances in short shorts and singing of off-color lyrics. Then came the strip dances. I began to get apprehensive again. I had seen little female skin between the neck and knees in my life and I was not eager for such exposure in a public place. As the skits unfolded I looked, then embarrassed, looked away. My friend John was taking it all in. While considerable bare skin was exposed the vital parts were not visible. I certainly didn't feel that I came of age through this visit. I was more turned off than on, though I loved the parts with music, but I never again visited a live burlesque show.

The day came for our departure home. We were a coterie of country boys now exposed to a city of consequence. It was a new experience and expanded our horizons. Most of us, however, I think, were ready to return to our country and village homes. Many slept on the 400-mile return trip.

After the war the prices of farm animals with price controls lifted shot upward rapidly. It was a good time to be farming. At that time I owned two New Hampshire sows and a Hereford heifer which I purchased from my uncle. I also purchased the feed. I had a few litters of pigs and a calf by the heifer. When I left for Harding College I sold off my breeding stock at the Thayer livestock auction. The breeding females brought enough so that I managed to make $2000 from my livestock operations. By making that much it was possible for me to apply for an award labeled Missouri State Farmer. I had to take an exam, write an essay, and report my expenses and profits from my farm projects. In the summer I received a certificate from the Missouri FFA organization. I was the first from the Alton chapter to secure this status. I was pleased with this attainment. I didn't mention it much, however, when I went to college. Not many of my college peers were from the farm, and they weren't impressed.

A COMMITMENT

From the age ten on I gave consideration to being baptized for the remission of sins. I considered myself basically a good person. I thought I shaped up pretty well. I did not play marbles for "keeps." I studiously avoided telling lies, though on occasion I didn't speak up for the truth, and may have told a few white lies, but I prided myself in these being very few. I did not play cards so as to gamble, knew nothing about dancing, and was never around alcohol so as to be tempted. I did not smoke, even though I could have taken cigarettes from my grandfather's store without him knowing it. My brothers and I, on a few occasions, resorted to smoking dry grape vines while hiding in the woods where our parents couldn't see us. My friends were basically of the same disposition. I was a good student and a keeper of the rules. I had to watch my "P's" and "Q's" since Aunt Alice Taylor taught home economics in the school system at Thayer all during the time I progressed from grades one through eight. When I attended high school at Alton and stayed with Uncle Cleo, he was the vocational agriculture teacher. I knew I couldn't engage in anything at school without my aunt and uncle hearing about it. So I was generally rule abiding and moral.

I did, however, believe that if I became a Christian I had some changes to make. The conviction about these grew as I passed from fourteen, fifteen to sixteen. I needed to give more when the collection was passed. I was something of a miser and dreaded parting with my money. My grandfather paid me periodically, often with a silver dollar. In summers my uncle paid the magnificent sum of a dollar a day for working from sun up to sun down on his farms. But he provided room and meals. He paid the same to a full time adult farm worker and furnished a house. I also knew I had to take up reading the Scriptures. I read them from time to time, but not with a great deal of enthusiasm. Novels and movies seemed much more exciting.

But there were two problems which I knew had to be addressed. The first was off-color jokes. I heard such jokes from traveling salesmen in my grandfather's store, from men who worked on my uncle's farms at harvest times, and from some of my schoolmates. Around adults I mostly listened, wide eared. Around my male schoolmates in private I repeated several of the jokes, as they shared ones they had heard. On trips to high school basketball games some of my friends and I sat in the back of the bus away from the girls and exchanged dirty jokes. Though I had an eye for the girls I was too timid to muster up the courage to sit by one or suggest a date. By joining the boys of like disposition and cracking jokes I was let off the hook. I knew if I became a Christian I would have to clean up my act. I did not swear or use foul language. One can maneuver through even sex jokes and avoid most of the bad language.

The other matter had to do with sex itself. Sex was a mystery which was discussed occasionally, often by way of jokes. My friends for the most part were intrigued but only discussants not activists. These days were prior to the sex revolution when most teens were fearful of indulgence on the grounds of pregnancy, disease, and disdain afterward by their companion. My interest in sex was perhaps accelerated by my mother who intended the opposite. She was always concerned especially when we went swimming in the creek if there were girls anywhere near. We swam in long pants rather than in swimming trunks at her insistence. She grilled us if we had been out of her sight for a time. It made us wonder what it was all about. As I moved toward the teens the impulses were there. It was clear to me that they had to be repressed and certainly not acted upon.

As I passed through the teens I knew that if I became a Christian it would be a major decision. I wanted to be a person who was helpful. I wanted to be a faithful reader of the Scriptures. I wanted to study for deeper spiritual insight. I felt that even with the changes in our churches, there was still too much focus on what was wrong with people in the sects, too much argument over inconsequential matters, too much preference for disputations instead of Christian action, and too much hypocrisy. A Christian needed to be a person of prayer, of kindness, of Biblical knowledge, and totally committed. He had to avoid the temptations into which I had to some degree plunged.[1]

In the summer of 1946, my two brothers, Glenn and Owen, a cousin, Don Beatty, and I discussed being baptized at the summer meeting in Thayer. We made up our mind as to what night it would be. The apprehensive moment came. I was ready, but I feared the public display. The invitation song commenced, "Are you washed in the blood of the lamb?" My heart raced, my breath grew short, and my palms perspired as they had many times in the past when I contemplated walking up the aisle. But this time I had committed myself not only to the Lord, but to my companions. We cleared the long seat and made our way to the front. When the song ceased, we stood one after the other before the congregation and confessed that Jesus is the Christ the Son of the living God. People seemed pleased but there was little public display. That was our way. A person or two dropped by and said, "Thomas, we are pleased that you have taken this step." We drove from the church building home to pick up a change of clothing then headed toward the deep pool in Warm Fork Creek north of town which was also our swimming hole. Cars drove to the creek bank. The headlights were directed downward. The beams crossed the stream and provided adequate illumination as the preacher plunged us beneath the waters in the name of the Father, of the Son, and the Holy Spirit. It was a new day. I had now taken the step I had longed to take for at least four years.

---

1. For additional in insights into my religious background see: Olbricht, "The Arrival of the Churches of Christ,75–88; Olbricht, "Restoration Revivalism, 88–108; Olbricht, *Reflections on My Life*.

My baptism occurred shortly before the commencement of my senior year in high school. I would have been fearful had I thought my school companions would learn of my decision. But I went to high school at Alton 17 miles away. My brothers and Don went to school in Thayer. There was not a Church of Christ in Alton, though there was one in the country about four miles out—Hickory Grove. I didn't have to worry. My secret was safe. I could work out the details of my new life without taunting from friends. I became a person of regular prayer. I determined to read through the Bible.

A MAJOR PROJECT

I learned early not to value knowledge simply for it own sake as did a dilettante. My Alton, MO, high school principal, Kenneth Ogle, was enamored with science, but he was a man of action. He decided that our senior science class would build a gymnasium score board. In 1946 the Alton, MO High School was basically a two-sports school, volleyball for the girls and basketball for the boys. We had just come through a depression and a war, and our school board didn't think we could afford the luxury of a commercial score board. Under Ogle's direction our science class set out to build a scoreboard depending upon plans he had ordered. We started with a 4 by 8 piece of plywood and cut holes on the left for the home team in two columns o through 9 and on the right identical holes for the visitors. A small bulb went behind each hole comprising 20 in all. We also had holes to indicate quarters and the time remaining. We didn't worry about scores higher than two digits because a huge high school basketball score was 40. This was before the 24-second shot clock and a team could dribble the whole game away should it desire. The control board consisted of switches that rotated o through 9, one for each set of lights. We had a transformer to reduce the current so that thin wires from the control board to the score board were bound together as a cable. After about a month we had it ready. We plugged it in and incredibly it worked. Whatever we learned of electricity and circuits we put to use and changed our own score-reporting world. From this experience I also learned what became even more important for me, the value of mentoring. Ogle worked closely with us on the project. I was sometimes asked to take charge when he was gone. Through this project I discovered the gratification that accompanies the achieving of a goal with others and of exercising leadership when called upon.

Missouri Memories, 1934–1947
MUSIC

I loved to sing, so I was involved in whatever chorus existed. The high school had a music teacher, Mrs. McClelland. Her husband owned the only drugstore in town and was a pharmacist. He was a distant relative. During the war the most we did was prepare a Christmas Cantata which we presented on a special December night. We also sang a time or two in the school assemblies and for graduation. After the war Mrs. McClelland decided to produce a Negro Minstrel. This was before the days of racial political correctness. Minstrels were popular in vaudeville earlier and continued to be produced in high schools until the early 1960s. No African-Americans lived in Oregon County, but all in the minstrels had black faces created by burnt cork and cold cream. Roles were often designed for parody. I played a Negro woman. Proper padding was placed in my dress to provide an authentic profile. I was involved in skits where jokes were told. I still recall some of the jokes. In one I was told by my "boyfriend" that he had a cow that produced buttermilk. I expressed my amazement. "How can a cow give buttermilk" I asked. He responded, "How can a cow give anything but her milk?" Then I told of the hen where for some reason an orange made its way into her nest. One of her chicks said to another, "Look at the orange momma laid." Our minstrel was eminently successful. We produced it on two different nights.

Our chorus sang for our 1947 graduation. One of our songs was the "Battle Hymn of the Republic." I was asked by Mrs. McClelland to sing a later verse as a solo with the chorus humming in the background.

> In the beauty of the lilies Christ was born across the sea,
> With a glory in His bosom that transfigures you and me:
> As He died to make men holy, let us die to make men free;
> While God is marching on.

I was honored since it was unusual in my time in the chorus to include a soloist especially a male.

In my last two years of high school our class composition changed with perhaps a dozen veterans returning to finish high school. One in my class was Leroy Chronister whose parents lived on a farm southeast of Alton. His family, Czech immigrants, played musical instruments and frequented country hoedowns. Hoedowns were popular though I never went to one. They occurred in country school houses and even in the yards of private dwellings in good weather. In fact the Grand Ole Opry was conceived by

George D. Hay when he came to Mammoth Spring in 1919 to attend a funeral. He heard of a country hoedown the night before on the Missouri border east of Mammoth. When the Orpry first aired in 1927 Hays declared that his decision to air the Opry was sparked by that hoedown. Chronister was an accomplished fiddler and mandolin player and had played in various informal gatherings while in the army. He discovered another high school student who could accompany him on a guitar so they started playing for about thirty minutes in the gymnasium during the noon hour. A crowd of forty or fifty usually gathered to hear them. Their signature piece was "Down Yonder" which they played as they began and ended. My Uncle Cleo had bought a mandolin a few years earlier thinking he would learn to play since he loved the mandolin so much. He had played the ukulele and sang as a college student. He loved to hear Leroy play and was almost always at the sessions. He gave Leroy his mandolin since he decided he would never use it.

DATING

I didn't do much dating in high school but a couple of girls caught my attention. My junior year I met Joy Woodring. Her family lived east near the Eleven Point River in a river camp cabin and were considered ne'er do well by my aunt. They were also perceived to be unstable since they moved back and forth to California to find work. Joy was about my height. I met her a time or two at the theatre on Saturday afternoon. One time I received permission from my uncle to borrow the pickup so as to take her home. We were, however, both rather stand offish and I didn't so much as try to hold her hand. My aunt tried to dissuade me from dating her, saying that she looked more like a boy than a girl. It was true that her clothes weren't exactly feminine though she wore dresses since girls did not wear slacks to class in those years. After my junior year she moved back to California.

One of the teachers had a daughter named Norma Jean Hardin and the teacher was interested in promoting male/female high school relationships. She started having gatherings at her house on Saturday night. She invited an equal number of boys and girls. It turned out that I was paired with a fairly good-looking redhead named Corrine Walters. I had talked to her some, but we hadn't made any effort to date. The night activities consisted of various games one of which was a version of post office, but one was only to kiss the girl with whom one was paired. Since the game was played in the yard after dark, at the time for the kiss the couple went behind a large tree. It finally happened that Corinne and I were to go behind the tree. My family wasn't kissy. I had never been kissed to my knowledge nor had I tried to kiss anyone. But I had seen kisses in movies so I thought I could carry it off. I'm not sure whether Corinne had ever been kissed but if so she was not very helpful. We didn't try to hug but just faced each other. It was dark enough that I could not see her that well, and it may have been that I had my eyes closed. Anyway my lips did not connect with her mouth, but with her cheek and she did not help direct her lips to mine. I was a bit embarrassed and didn't make a second try. That was my only attempt at kissing a girl in those high school years.

The night after graduation there was something of a party at school. I arranged to drive Corrine home along with another couple. I knew the other girl better than I did Corrine. Her name was Mary Lou Johnson. Her boyfriend was a steady. I don't now remember his name. We all rode in the cab of the pickup and as was typical then, Mary Lou sat on her boyfriend's lap.

Normally the senior class took a day trip the last week of school. Our trip was a picnic at a campground just south of the bridge on the Eleven Point River east of Alton. I spent a bit of time with Corrine at the picnic, but we also talked with others so it wasn't a date. During the summer of 1947, Corrine worked on the telephone switchboard in Alton. I dropped by to talk with her a time or two, but we didn't date. Sometime in the summer I heard that she had dated a single man about twenty-five years old. I knew him somewhat and his family was distantly related as were a number of persons in our region. I also heard that Corrine thought I wasn't interested in her anymore. So I made a special trip to talk with her at the switchboard and tell her that I wanted to maintain our relationship. Soon afterward I was injured in logging and had to stay in bed for about a month. I never tried to talk with Corrine again after that.

By the summer of 1947, county fairs were reemerging with much energy since the returned veterans contributed expertise and dedication. The Oregon County fair was held at the Alton fair grounds northwest of the town. Uncle Cleo bought a buggy with four seats and one higher up in the front for the driver. I don't recall the make, but it was similar to a Ford buggy. He also bought an older mare to pull it. The exhibition of buggies was becoming popular at horse shows. Soon after the end of the war regular horse shows were launched in Alton and supported by my Uncle. We took the buggy to the fair, and alternately he and I drove around offering rides to those attending the fair. My riders were mostly girls my age and on one occasion Helen Dorris was among them.

One day, Mary Ann Taylor of Thayer—whose grandfather Peter Taylor was the brother of my grandfather, T. Shelt Taylor—arrived at the fair. We struck up a conversation. She was almost a year older than I and in the graduating class ahead of me. We decided to board several of the rides together, and a bit of chemistry seemed to be emerging. My mother was also present and observed us for a time. After we ended our rides and I went back to the buggy she came over to talk with me. "Now Thomas, you mustn't get interested in Mary Ann because after all she is your cousin." I had heard mother lecture before on how if people marry their relatives defective genes result, leading to mental defects and insanity. I smiled and told her I didn't think that just because we had hit it off and taken a few rides that marriage was on the horizon.

At the end of the war many service men returned as experienced pilots. County fairs soon were flooded with barnstorming veterans usually flying a small Piper Cub. A barnstormer from the region flew from an air strip located near the Alton fair ground. After receiving two dollars the pilot took passengers for a thirty-minute ride showing them buildings in the town and outlying areas. I had not yet been up in a plane and wanted to try it. I was a bit fearful, however, because I was inflicted with car sickness at a younger age. It was a calm day, however, and I thought I could manage. I asked the pilot if he would fly me to Thayer and land on my grandfather's recently mowed alfalfa field. A straight section on the farm was regularly used as a landing strip for barnstormers. He told me he would take me to Thayer for three dollars. The next day I told my parents and grandparents I was going to arrive by air. The flight was smooth, and I discouraged the pilot from doing loops and flying upside down. We did a few less demanding maneuvers. We landed, I got out and could walk fairly normal though with a bit of nausea. The pilot headed down the runway and flew back to Alton. That was my introduction to flying at the ripe age of seventeen. I liked flying, but I decided then I would never take flying lessons.

LOGGING

South of Uncle Cleo's ranch was a farm of a hundred sixty acres that came up for sale that was contiguous with the ranch. It had some better farmland than on the ranch and had at least forty acres of oak trees that had never been cut. These could be cut and sold for the asking price of the farm. Uncle Cleo therefore bought the farm. He knew a nearby man with a horse who could skid the logs to a place where they would be loaded on a truck and hauled to a saw mill about three miles away. My brother Glenn and I had helped saw up a number of trees for fire wood on the farm east of Alton where Uncle Cleo lived. He decided that Glenn and I should cut saw logs in the summer of 1947 rather than pursue other farm activities. We cut for a week and Uncle Cleo was pleased with our accomplishments. We were forewarned to be extremely careful in felling a slanting tree since they tended to split up and lash back at those sawing. The second week we ran across a leaning oak tree that contained a couple of excellent logs about two feet in diameter. We knew it might be dangerous, and therefore we made a deep notch in the tree somewhat higher up thinking that would keep it from splitting. We preceded then to saw it down. We were very leery and ready to run in case it started splitting. Despite our precautions the tree started spitting and coming at me rapidly. I quickly moved away but as it fell it hit me on the shoulder and knocked me down. I ended up with my left foot under the tree. The ground was relatively soft, and it didn't take long to remove my foot, but it had been crushed by the tree. Glenn got a hold of our uncle, and he took me to the doctor. The foot was very painful, and I could no longer walk on it. The doctor declared that no bones were broken, but the foot had been crushed enough that the danger was that I could get gangrene. My parents and grandfather were especially concerned because one of my grandfather's brothers had had a leg crushed by a tree and died of gangrene. I was told that I would have to stay in bed for three weeks and watch my foot very carefully for any signs of gangrene. The accident ended my career as a logging man. I was back again walking as before in a month but for a time with a bit of a limp. I finished the summer involved in other sorts of farm activities.

CONCLUSION

My high school years were hardly drama filled, but enough so that I eagerly awaited whatever each new day brought. My experiences were many and varied. I both experienced much and learned much. Uncle Cleo was a great mentor. My parents and grandparents were supportive. My siblings and friends participated along the way, and we enjoyed our time together.

Peace

My days sometimes brought vicissitudes and problems, but they were manageable since major forces of evil were missing in our small Ozark towns and countryside in that day and age. I successfully navigated times of war and peace in my high school years. When I left for college I strongly felt I could cope with whatever should arise. In fact my major problem the first semester was overcoming home sickness. I knew what I was doing and why in my high school years. After I was in college for a time I was no longer as confident, and in fact my goals began to change. But I had taken my boot training in the Ozarks, and I was adequately prepared to face the future whatever its course.

Afterword

BROOKS BLEVINS, DEPARTMENT OF HISTORY,
MISSOURI STATE UNIVERSITY, SPRINGFIELD, MISSOURI

It's different, but probably not as much as we think. I suppose you could call this my mantra for the Ozarks—of the present and the past. The region has often been depicted as a backward land forgotten by time, as a place so tied to the past that people from other parts of the country could come here to see how their ancestors lived. While it isn't, and wasn't, Manhattan or Kansas City, or even Springfield, the Ozarks of south central Missouri probably isn't, and wasn't, as unlike the rest of the country as we may be tempted to believe.

Tom Olbricht's interesting and informative memoir of his "boot camp" upbringing in Oregon County describes a place that certainly would have seemed foreign to a New Yorker or a Chicagoan in the 1930s and 1940s—he was after all sixteen years old and a senior in high school before he ever saw a traffic light. But the reader can follow the broad contours of American small-town and rural life in these pages—the Depression-era and wartime world of Saturday picture shows, Philco radios, drugstore sodas, Sunday dinners, gospel meetings, homemade fishing poles, visits from Santa Claus, kite flying, rationing, hog slopping, cow milking, and halting attempts at sparking. It's a story that many Americans from Tom's generation will find familiar, a story that will almost certainly trigger feelings of nostalgia among those of us who are younger. In spite of the material and social limitations of the time and place, Oregon County in the Depression and war years was a good place to grow up; it was a place that helped make Tom Olbricht the remarkable person that he is.

Afterword

In some ways, though, the story of the Olbricht family diverges from the standard story of the Ozarks. In a place assumed to be populated by descendants of the Scots-Irish who made their way to the hills of Missouri and Arkansas from Tennessee and Kentucky, Tom grew up with German-born grandparents and a father who spent his formative and young adult years on the plains of Nebraska. In a place that still today can boast of comparatively few college-educated persons—and in those days almost none—Tom not only had a mother who was a college graduate, but he was reared in a family (the Taylors) remarkably devoted to higher education. In a place seemingly dominated by the emotional revivalism of Baptists, Methodists, and Pentecostals, Tom grew up in the reasoned, explicatory atmosphere of the Churches of Christ. In a time and place when many in the Ozarks continued to come to town in horse-drawn wagons, Tom spent his early years beside a busy U.S. highway with a grandfather who made his living off the drivers motoring through the Ozarks. And he played golf in his grandfather's pasture, for goodness sake.

His early life nicely straddled the divide between small town and country. His experiences gave him an appreciation for the advantages and challenges each provided and likely prevented him from ever feeling trapped in one world or the other. Of course, lots of other people with similar upbringings failed to achieve the successes that Tom has achieved and failed to impact the world around them as Tom has done. So some of this story simply illustrates the ability of an extraordinary soul to make the most of what he has at hand, to take from the world that which is enriching, to extract value from the lessons others ignore. Tom Olbricht is rightly proud of his heritage in rural Oregon County, Missouri—and Oregon County should be proud that it can claim such a son as its own.

Grandparents T. Shelt and Myrtle Taylor, Barbara Taylor Sorrell and daughter

Grandparents Taylor house, Thayer, MO

T. Shelt Taylor gas station and house

Grandparents Henry and Bertha Olbricht, Passport

Tom and Nedra Olbricht and Cats

Owen, Tom (Age 7), Glenn Olbricht

Second Grade, Thayer. Tom top row tallest toward right

Thayer Elementary School

Thayer, MO, Main Street

Thayer, MO, Main Street

The house where Tom was born, abandoned by the time the picture was taken

Ben J. and Agnes Taylor Olbricht, Tom's parents

House of Cleo Taylor, Alton, MO. Tom lived there during high school years

Alton, MO, Oregon County Courthouse

Grand Gulf west of Thayer, MO

Greer Spring, Northeast of Alton, MO

The Taylor Family
<u>Front row</u>: Ted Taylor, Myrtle Taylor, Bertha Taylor Lewis,
Dessie Martin, Jean Taylor, Jack Taylor
<u>Back row</u>: Ben Olbricht, Mabel Taylor, Norval Taylor, T. Shelt Taylor,
Dortha Taylor, Wellington Taylor, Bert Lewis, Cleo Taylor, Ova Taylor,
Alice Taylor Copenhagen, Ralph Copenhagen

Mabel Taylor, Barbara Ann Taylor (daughter of Cleo) Norval Taylor

Bertha Taylor Lewis

Cleo Taylor

Alice Taylor Copenhagen

Olbricht Family: Glenn, Ben, Owen, Agnes, Tom, Nedra

Tom, Alton High School Junior

Tom, Alton High Graduate

Tom and Hay on Cleo Taylor's pickup, High School Senior

Alton, MO High School Building

Bibliography

Blower, Paul M. et al., eds, *Encyclopedia of the Stone-Campbell Movement.* Anthony L. Dunnavant, Douglas A. Foster, D. Newell Williams, Grand Rapids: Eerdmans, 2004.

Blumhofer, Edith and Randall Balmer, eds., *Modern Christian Revivals.* Urbana: University of Illinois Press, 1993.

Boles, John B., *The Great Revival: Beginnings of The Bible Belt.* Lexington, Ky.: University Press of Kentucky, 1996.

Brents, T. W., *The Gospel Plan of Salvation.* Cincinnati: Bosworth, Chase and Hall, 1874.

Bruce, Dickson D., Jr., *And They All Sang Hallelujah: Plain-Folk Camp-Meeting Religion, 1800–1845.* Knoxville: University of Tennessee Press, 1974.

Burgess, Stanley, "Perspectives on the sacred: Religion in the Ozarks," *Ozarks Watch*, II, 2, 1988.

Churchill, Craig, "Creath, Jacob, Jr.," *The Encyclopedia of the Stone-Campbell Movement.* 250–51, eds. Paul M. Blowers, et al.

Conkin, Paul, *Cane Ridge: America's Pentecost.* Madison, WI: University of Wisconsin Press, 1990.

Donan, Philip, *Memoir of Jacob Creath, Jr.* Cincinnati: R. W. Carroll & Co, 1872.

Eslinger, Ellen, *Citizens: The Social Origins of Camp Meeting Revivalism.* Knoxville, The University of Tennessee Press, 1999.

Foreman, Lawton Durant, and Alta Payne, *The Life and Works of Benjamin Marcus Bogard.* Little Rock, Bogard Publications, 1965.

Garrison, Winfred Ernest and Alfred T. DeGroot, *The Disciples of Christ: A History.* St. Louis: The Bethany Press, 1948.

Gaustad, Edwin S., *The Great Awakening in New England.* Gloucester, Mass: P. Smith, 1965.

Gilmore, Robert K., Ozark Baptizings, *Hangings, and Other Diversions: Theatrical Folkways of Rural Missouri, 1885–1910.* Norman: University of Oklahoma Press, 1984.

Halvorson, Peter L. and William M. Newman, *Atlas of Religious Change in America.* Atlanta: Glenmary Research Center, 1994.

Hambrick-Stowe, Charles E., *Charles G. Finney and the Spirit of American Evangelicalism.* Grand Rapids, MI: W.B. Eerdmans Pub. Co., 1996.

Hill, Samuel S., *One Name but Several Faces: Variety in Popular Christian Denominations in Southern History.* Athens, GA: University of Georgia Press, 1996.

Bibliography

Holifield, Brooks E., *Era of Persuasion : American Thought and Culture, 1521–1680*. Boston: Twayne Publishers, 1989.

Hughes, Richard T., *Reviving the Ancient Faith: The Story of Churches of Christ in America*. Grand Rapids: Wm. B. Eerdmans, 1996.

Johnson, Charles A., *The Frontier Camp Meeting: Religion's Harvest Time*. Dallas: Southern Methodist University Press, 1955.

Lemmons, Reuel, "A Little Bit of History," *Firm Foundation*. October 18, 1966.

Leonard, Bill J., ed., *Christianity in Appalachia: Profiles in Regional Pluralism*. 1st ed. Knoxville: University of Tennessee Press, 1999.

Macfarlan, Duncan, *The revivals of the Eighteenth Century, Particularly at Cambuslang : with three Sermons by the Rev. George Whitefield, taken in short hand / compiled from original manuscripts and contemporary publications*. Wheaton: Richard Owen Roberts, 1980.

McClymond, Michael, ed., *Encyclopedia of Religious Revivals in America*. Westport, CT: Greenwood Press, 2007.

McLoughlin, Jr., William G., *Modern Revivalism: Charles Grandison Finney to Billy Graham*. New York: Ronald Press, 1959.

Moore, W. T., ed., "Winthrop H. Hopson," *Living Pulpit of the Christian Church*. Cincinnati: R. W. Carroll & Co., Publishers, 1871.

Morgan, Boyd E., *Arkansas Angels*. Paragould, AR: College Bookstore & Press, 1967.

Olbricht, Thomas H, *Hearing God's Voice: My Life with Scriptures in Churches of Christ*. ACU Press, 1996.

Olbricht, Thomas H. "Prayer Meeting," *Dictionary of Christianity in America*. Daniel C. Reid, et al., eds.

Olbricht, Thomas H., "Churches of Christ," *Encyclopedia of the Stone-Campbell Movement*. eds. Paul M. Blowers, et al.

Olbricht, Thomas H., "Recalling Ozarks Past: Winter 1936," *OzarksWatch*, Series 2, III, 2.

Olbricht, Thomas H., "Restoration Revivalism in Oregon Country, Missouri, and Fulton County, Arkansas, 1930–1950" *Elder Mountain:A Journal of Ozarks Studies*. Vol. 4, 2012.

Olbricht, Thomas H., "The Arrival of the Churches of Christ in Randolph & Fulton Counties, Arkansas, and in Oregon Country Missouri," *OzarksWatch*, Series 2, III, 1.

Olbricht, Thomas H., "The Holy Spirit in the Early Restoration Movement," *Stone-Campbell Journal*. 7:2004.

Olbricht, Thomas H., "The Invitation—A Survey" *Restoration Quarterly*. 5:1, 1961.

Olbricht, Thomas H., *Reflections on My Life in the Kingdom and the Academy*. Eugene, OR: Wipf and Stock, 2012.

Rafferty, Milton D., *The Ozarks: Land and Life*, 2nd edition. Fayetteville: The University of Arkansas Press, 2001.

Reid, Daniel C., et al., eds., *Dictionary of Christianity in America*. Robert D. Linder, Bruce L. Shelley, Harry S. Stout, Downers Grove, IL: InterVarsity, 1990.

Schmidt, Leigh Eric, *Holy Fair: Scotland and the Making of American Revivalism*. Grand Rapids: W.B. Eerdmans Pub., 2001.

Scott, Walter *The Evangelist*. 1832.

Scott, Walter, *The Gospel Restored. A Discourse of the True Gospel of Jesus Christ, in which the Facts, Principles, Duties, and Privileges of Christianity are Arranged, Defined, and Discussed, and the Gospel in its various Parts Shown to be Adapted to the Nature and Necessities of Man in his Present Condition*. Cincinnati: Ormsby H. Donogh, 1836.

Bibliography

Sears, Lloyd Cline, *The Eyes of Jehovah: The Life and Faith of James Alexander Harding*. Nashville: Gospel Advocate Company, 1970.

Shelly, B. L., "James McGready," *Dictionary of Christianity in America*. Reid, Daniel C., et al., eds.

Smith, Loyd L., "Bynum Black," *Gospel Preachers of Yesteryear*. Self Published, 1986.

Srygley, F. D., *Biographies and Sermons*. Nashville: The Gospel Advocate Company, Reprint 1961.

Stone, Barton W., *A Short History of the Life of Barton W. Stone Written by Himself* 1847. St. Louis, Mo.: The Bethany Press, 1954.

Travis, William G., "Protestant Revivalism," *Dictionary of Christianity in America*. Daniel C. Reid, et al., eds.

Weisberger, Bernard A., *They Gathered at the River: The Story of the Great Revivalists and Their Impact upon Religion in America*. Boston: Little, Brown and Company, 1958.

Wilson, Michael L., *Arkansas Christians: A History of the Restoration Movement in Randolph County, Arkansas, 1800–1995*. Delight, AR: Gospel Light Publishing Company, 1997.

Name Index

Acuff, Roy, 65
Albin, Craig, x
Alden, John, 31
Allen, Johnny, 116
Amos and Andy, 65
Autry, Gene, 102, 109

Balmer, Randall, 90, 149
Barker, Arthur, 52
Barker, Fred, 52
Barker, Herman, 52
Barker, Lloyd, 52
Barker, Ma, 52
Barnes, Dr., 3, 8
Barton, Joe, 123
Barton, John, 123
Beatty, Don, 55, 126
Benny, Jack, 65
Berry, Wendell, xii
Bittner, Robert, 8
Black, Bynum, 75, 85–86
Black, Elic, 85
Black, Harriet, 85
Blevins, Brooks, iii, vii ix–x, 89, 135–36
Blowers, Paul M., 72, 79, 149, 150
Blue, Joe H., 86–88
Blue, Mary Montgomery, 87
Blumhofer, Edith, 149
Bogard, Ben M., 86, 149
Boles, John B., 90, 149
Boone, Daniel, 84
Borden, E. M., 76
Boughnou, 77–78

Brents, T. W., 87, 96, 149
Brewer, G. C., 96
Brumley, Albert E., 110
Burgess, Stanley, 90, 149

Calhoun, Hall, 96
Calvin, John, 89, 94
Campbell, Alexander, 4, 72, 74–75, 78, 81. 89, 92, 94–95, 149–50
Campbell, Thomas, 74
Carson, Kit, 89
Carter Family, 65
Cartright family, 77
Chappell, Ella Lord, 79
Chronister, Leroy, 128–29
Churchill, Craig, 79, 149
Conkin, Paul, 90, 149
Copenhagen, Ralph, 144
Cratchit, Bob, 31
Creath, Jacob, JR, 79, 149

Daller, Forrest, 66
Davis, Gladys, 63
Dawson, Gerald, 12
Dawson, Monroe, 11
Dawson, Mrs., 11
Deffenbaugh, Don, 81
DeGroot, Alfred T., 78, 149
Dell, Alice Sue, 60
Dell, Mary Lou, 60
Dell, Ray, 60
Dickson, D. Bruce, Jr., 149
Dinesen, Izak, xi

Name Index

Donan, Philip, 149
Dorris, Gordon, 111
Dorris, Helen, 111. 131
Douglas, Lloyd C., 11
Dubois, Drew, 82
Dubois, J. Paul, 67
Dunnavant, Anthony L., 149
Dunsmore Brothers, 53
Dunsmore, Albert, 34
Dunsmore, Bynum, 23–24, 35 38, 58, 61, 100
Dunsmore, James Ray, 23, 35, 55, 58, 61, 65, 100, 112
Dunsmore, Lavina, 21
Dunsmore, Lucy, 21, 63
Dunsmore, Opal Martin, 23, 35, 61, 100
Dunsmore, Roy, 66

Edison, Thomas A., xii, 20
Edwards, Jonathan, 90–91
English, Maggie, 85
English, Nancy Taylor, 85
English, Will, 85
Eslinger, Ellen, 91, 149
Evans, James A., 78
Evans, Max H., x, 77
Evans, William Nelson, 78

Fanning, Tolbert, 4, 73
Felix the Cat, 40, 49
Finney, Charles Grandison, 92–93, 149, 150
Ford, Henry, 20
Foreman, Lawton Durant, 86, 149
Foster, Douglas A., 149
Francke, August Hermann, 90
Freylinghausen, Theodore, 90
Friedman, Robert, x
Fry, Jane, 82
Fry, John L., 82–83, 86
Fry, Leondus, 82

Garrison, Winfred Ernest, 78, 149
Gaustad, Edwin S., 91, 149
George and Garner preachers, 87
Gilmore, Robert K., 95, 149
Gingerich, Margaret, 64

Graham, Billy, 90, 150
Green, Martha (Mattie) Dunsmore, 75, 95
Gretel, 19
Griffith, Hilton, 53
Griffith, Tom, 81–82, 85
Gum, Ben, 115–16

Hackett, Dorris, 31
Hall, Donald, 70
Halvorson, Peter L. , 88, 149
Hambrick-Stowe, Charles E., 93. 149
Hansel, 19
Hardeman, N. B., 96
Hardin, Norma Jean, 129
Harding, James A., 83, 96. 151
Havens, Luther, 21
Hay, George D., 129
Henegar, Bill, x
Henegar, Patty, x
Hickok, Wild Bill, 109
Hicks family, 77
Hicks, Lewis, 61
Hicks, Rob, 9, 16, 20, 61
Hicks, Stella, 20, 61
Hill, Samuel S., 95, 149
Hinkle, boy, 18
Hodges, W. B., 63
Holifield, Brooks E., 83, 150
Holladay, Carl, xv
Holloway, Marshall, 81, 85
Holman, Jack, 111
Hopson, Winthrop H., 79, 150
Huffstedler family, 77
Hughes, Richard T., 95, 150
Hunter, Ben, 63
Hunter, Mabel, 63
Hurlbert, 19

James, Dellar, 49
James, Harriett, 81
James, Hellen Rose, 81
James, Isaac, 82
Jiggs and Maggie, 40
Johnson, Charles A. , 91, 150
Johnson, Mary Lou, 130
Johnson, Ned, 119
Jones, Abner, 74–75, 80–81

Name Index

Josh, Uncle, 39

Kamm, Edward, 67–68
Karpis, Alvin "Creepy", 52
Katzenjammer Kids, 40
Keeble, Marshall, 96
Kellett, Lum, 82
Kelly, Roy C., 52
Kennedy, John F., 118
Kiel, Orville, 70

Lamarr, Hedy, 63
Langley, Richard Livingston, 5
Larimore, T. B., 4, 73, 96
Lemmons, Amos J., 84
Lemmons, Benjamin Monroe, 81. 84–85
Lemmons, John M., 84, 86
Lemmons, Reuel, 76, 77, 150
Lemmons, Walter F., 86
Leonard, Bill J., 95, 150
Lewis, Bert, 144
Lipscomb, David, 73, 96
Little Abner, 40
Longfellow, Henry Wadsworth, 19

Macfarlan, Duncan, 91, 150
Mainprize, Jack, 55, 65–67
Martin, Dessie, 9, 144
Martin, Jim, 9, 23–24, 82
Martin, Richard, 60
McClelland, Mrs., 128
McClymond, Michael, 150
McGee, Fibber and Molly, 65
McGill, James R., 76
McGill, Nedra Olbricht, 3, 8, 14, 17, 19–21, 25–26, 35, 54, 57, 62, 76, 100, 139, 146
McGinness, Cleone, x
McGready, James, 91, 151
McLoughlin, William G., 90, 150
Millsap, Betty, 110
Millsap, Billy, 110
Minnie Pearl, 65
Mix, Tom, 109
Moody, Dwight L., 98
Moody, L. N., 49
Moore, W. T., 79, 150

Morgan, Boyd, 77, 81–87, 150
Morris, Jesse, 5
Mueller, George, 83
Mullins, Pricilla, 31
Murray, Ed, 51

Newman, William M., 88, 149
Nichol, C. R., 96
Norman, M. George, 4–5

O'Kelly, James, 74, 81
Ogle, Kenneth, 127
Olbricht, Agnes Taylor, ix, 8, 11–13, 19–22, 25, 75, 100, 142, 146 and *passim*
Olbricht, Benjamin, 39–40
Olbricht, Benjamin J., 8, 14–19, 25, 73, 75, 100–101, 142, 144. 146 and *passim*
Olbricht, Bertha Lange, 6, 36–37, 39, 79, 138
Olbricht, Erika M., x
Olbricht, Frank, 49
Olbricht, Glenn C., 8, 14, 18–20, 25–26, 46, 48, 65, 76, 100, 105, 116, 126, 132, 139, 146
Olbricht, Henry, 6–10, 23, 30, 36–38, 40, 72, 101, 138
Olbricht, Joseph, 37, 73
Olbricht, Katherine Eich, 37, 79
Olbricht, Matilda Lange, 37
Olbricht, Minnie, 49
Olbricht, Owen D., x, 8, 14. 18–20, 25–26, 30–31, 46, 48, 65. 76, 79, 100, 105, 116, 126, 139, 146
Olbricht, Theodore, 13, 37–38
Olbricht, Vernie, 37–39

Pace family, 77
Pack, T. T., 83
Patton, General George S., 108. 118
Pauli, Adolph, 38
Pauli, Lucy Dunsmore, 38
Payne, Alta, 86, 149
Perrin, Jim, 81, 85
Pingleton, Bernadine, 18
Powell, Billy, 21
Powell, Nadine, 21

Name Index

Powell, Ruby, 21
Prewitt, Albert, 33, 68–70, 102–3. 115, 119
Prewitt, Bertha Johnson, 112, 119
Prewitt. Elmer, 102–3
Prewitt. Perry, 103
Prince, Thomas, 91
Pulley, Kathy J., ii, vii, ix-xv

Queen Mary (Bloody), 21

Rafferty, Milton D., 89, 150
Rand, Sally, 123
Rebecca of Sunnybrook Farm, 20
Risner, Arden, 123
Rogers, Buck, 40
Rogers, J. W., 83
Rogers, Roy, 102, 109
Rogers, Will, 11
Roosevelt, Franklin D., 43–44, 106
Roosevelt, Theodore, 102
Rose, Daniel, 80–81, 84
Rose, Daniel Darius, 80–81
Rose, Napoleon Bonaparte, 81–82
Rover Boys, 20

Sauser, Ernest, 7, 17, 37–38, 59, 61–62
Sauser, Evelyn, 61
Sauser, Grace, 61
Sauser, Pearl Dunsmore, 36, 59, 61
Sauser, Walter, 61–62
Schmidt, Leigh Eric, 91, 150
Scott, Walter, 94–95, 150
Sears, Lloyd Cline, 96, 151
Seuell, John C., 104
Sheldon, Charles, xii, 11
Shelly, B. L., 91, 151
Simmons, Sammy, 32
Simpson, Louis, 119–20
Smalzbauer, John, x, 89
Smith, Elias, 74–75, 80–81
Smith, Joseph, 86
Smith, Loyd L., 151
Smith, Slats, 41
Soelle, Dorothee, xiv
Spener, Philip Jacob , 90
Srygley, F. D., 151
Standish, Miles, 31

Stevenson, Robert Lewis, 19
Steward, Jimmy, 63
Stone, Barton W., 72, 74–75, 77–78, 80, 82, 92, 94–95, 149–50

Talley, Mary Ann Taylor, 4, 79, 131
Taylor, Amy AnthumWaits, 4–6, 73, 79
Taylor, Barbara Ann Sorrell, 100, 137, 144
Taylor, Calvin, 49
Taylor, Cleo S., ix-x, xii, 2, 9, 15, 23–24, 33, 35, 42, 44, 46, 54–55, 58, 61, 68, 79, 95, 100, 102–3, 107, 111–15, 120–22, 125, 129–32, 142, 144, 145, 147
Taylor, Dortha Rideout, 5, 52, 63–64, 104, 144
Taylor, Jack, 144
Taylor, Jean, 144
Taylor, Jim Henry, 82
Taylor, John Moody, 4–6, 49, 73, 79, 81–82
Taylor, John preacher, 4
Taylor, Mabel Lewis, 35, 48, 61, 144–45
Taylor, Mary Almanza Rose, 81
Taylor, Myrtle Dunsmore, v, 8, 10, 33–35, 46, 75, 86, 100, 137, 144 and *passim*
Taylor, Norval, ix-x, 16, 20, 27, 33, 35, 48, 61, 103–4, 107, 144–45
Taylor, Ova Martin, xiv, 9, 23–24, 36, 44, 61, 100, 103, 144
Taylor, Simion Peter, 81–82, 131
Taylor, Ted, 104, 144
Taylor, Thomas, 5
Taylor, Thomas Shelton, v, 4–5, 7–10, 23, 32, 35–36, 46, 68, 73, 75–76, 79, 81–82, 84–86, 100, 102, 131, 137–38, 144 and *passim*
Taylor, Wellington Thomas, ix-x, 4–5, 33–34, 40–41, 46, 49. 52–54, 58, 63–65, 69, 79, 103–4, 144
Thomas, Lowell, 18
Tidd, Mark, 20
Tiny Tim, 31
Toby Tent Shows, 50
Tolstoy, Leo, 100
Tracey, Dick, 40

156

Name Index

Travis, William G., 77
Van Bauer family, 77

Waits, Judah Hester, 4
Waits, Martha Ann, 5
Waits, Simeon C., 4
Waits, Simon C., Jr., 5
Wallace, Cled, 76
Wallace, Foy E., Jr., 96
Wallace, G. K., 72, 76, 96–99
Wallace, Glenn, 96
Walters, Corinne, 129–30

Ward (a Mormon), 86
Webber, Jack, 18
Weisberger, Bernard A. , 93, 151
Whitefield, George, 91, 150
Whiteside, R. L., 96
Williams, D. Newell, 149
Wilson, Michael L., 76, 80, 84, 151
Woodring, Joy, 129

Zickefoose, Ben, 97
Zwingli, Huldrych, 89

www.ingramcontent.com/pod-product-compliance
Lightning Source LLC
Chambersburg PA
CBHW071429160426
43195CB00013B/1853